THE CHAOS THE TRINITY CREATED

CULMINATING IN

ISLAMIC TERRORISM

J. CHAPMAN

J. Chapman

◆ FriesenPress

Suite 300 - 990 Fort St
Victoria, BC, Canada, V8V 3K2
www.friesenpress.com

ISBN
978-1-4602-8356-1 (Hardcover)
978-1-4602-8357-8 (Paperback)
978-1-4602-8358-5 (eBook)

1. Religion, Christian Church, Canon & Ecclesiastical Law

Distributed to the trade by The Ingram Book Company

TABLE OF CONTENTS

PART 4- MORE CHAOS OR CONFUSION

PART 5 - SUMMARY

PART 6 - CONCLUSION

PREFACE

The purpose of this book is not to compare Muslims versus Christians, but to compare the books that each bases his beliefs on. While my opinion will become apparent, it is not my words that are important here, rather the principles or tenets of the books that create the beliefs of its followers that I want the reader to understand. This book is separated into six parts:

> Part 1 is an introduction to understanding the cause of Islamic terrorism.
>
> Part 2 will clarify what Christians and Muslim teach about God; first we look at the Bible because it predates the Qur'an, and then the Qur'an because it refers to the Bible. Also included will be excerpts from the books of six theologian's doctrines supporting the trinity, with explanatory comments.

Chapters one and two of Part 2 serve as the necessary foundation for the rest of this book.

Part 3 will compare the Bible to the doctrines of Catholicism, Mormonism, Jehovah's Witnesses, and Oneness Pentecostals.

Part 4 will explore two doctrinal differences among Christians.

Part 5 will be a summary.

Part 6 will be a conclusion and some reform ideas.

INTRODUCTION

There is a blind spot in the war on terrorism. That blind spot is the lack of knowledge of the root cause of Islamic terrorism: the beliefs of the Muslim terrorist that motivates them into thinking that violence is the answer.

Whether one believes in God or not, understanding what your neighbor believes, and why, is of paramount importance to peace in this ever-shrinking world. It is not enough to be tolerant of one another; we each must look at ourselves to see why the other – may or may not – tolerate us.

Resolving religious differences is not that difficult; examining our own beliefs is what we have been unwilling to do. Peace comes with a price: exhausted bloodshed, or life-giving education.

The text of this book is a simplified comparison of the verses found in the Bible and the Qur'an, the two books that the Christians and Muslims use respectively for the foundations of their beliefs. It is an effort to expose the misunderstandings of each religion's traditional teachings.

PART 1 - ISLAMIC TERRORISM

CHAPTER 1 – THE CAUSE

Muslims around the world are protesting. They have even called on the United Nations to institute blasphemy laws because they are of the conviction that their religion and prophet are being disrespected. Some Islamic fundamentalists take much more serious steps: terrorism.

One of the reasons that terrorism is increasing is that when the US President George W. Bush declared war against terrorism, some Muslims believed that President Bush had declared war against their religion, Islam.

Because the Muslim is instructed by the Qur'an to follow the teachings of Muhammad, who is described in the Qur'an as a man of perfect conduct, the West must look to the teachings of Muhammad in the Qur'an to understand why some Muslims become terrorists.

Few are aware of what the Qur'an propagates. The Islamic uprising can best be understood by the following three principles taken directly out of the Qur'an:

a. A Muslim is commanded to fight for his belief when it is challenged.

b. A Muslim is given the authority to kill those who do not submit to Islam (even children, because according to Islam, a Muslim and only a Muslim is considered innocent).

c. A Muslim is promised a reward in Paradise if he fights and dies for Islam.

The following is an incomplete list of verses taken contextually from Majid Fakhry's translation of the Qur'an, *An Interpretation of the Qur'an*.[1] The book cover states that the book has been "*Approved by Al-Azar University*." (Al-Azhar University, Cairo, Egypt)

- Fight those from among the People of the Book* [translator's footnote: * Jews and Christians] who do not believe in Allah and the Last Day, do not forbid what Allah and His Messenger have forbidden and do not profess the true religion, till they pay the poll tax out of hand and submissively.[2]

- Those who believe fight for the cause of Allah, and those who disbelieve fight on the behalf of the Devil.[3]

- Fight those of the unbelievers who are near to you and let them see how harsh you can be.[4]

- O Prophet, fight the unbelievers and the hypocrites and be stern with them. Their abode is Hell.[5]

1   Majid Fakhry, *An Interpretation of the Qur'an*, New York University Press, copyright 2000, 2004,

2   Qur'an ,chapter 9 vs. 29

3   Qur'an, 4:76

4   Qur'an, 9:123

5   Qur'an, 9:73

- O Prophet, urge the believers to fight.[6]

- You shall find others who wish to be secure from you and secure from their own people; yet, whenever they are called back to sedition* [translator's footnote: *polytheism] they plunge into it. If these do not keep away from you, nor offer you peace, nor hold their hands back, then seize them and kill them wherever you find them. Those, We [Allah] have given you clear authority over.[7]

- Indeed, the punishment of those who fight Allah and His Messenger and go around corrupting the land is to be killed, crucified. O believers, fear Allah and seek the means to win His Favor. Fight in His way so that you may prosper.[8]

- O Prophet, struggle with the unbelievers and the hypocrites, and deal harshly with them.[9]

- Muhammad is the Messenger of Allah and those who are with him are hard on the unbelievers.[10]

- When you meet the unbelievers, strike their necks till you have bloodied them.[11]

Amongst the general non-Islamic "unbelieving" population, adherents to Judaism and Christianity are specifically targeted as unbelievers. This is predominately because the Qur'an teaches that the holy books of the Jews and Christians were passed down by Allah, but have been corrupted by both groups. Much of the Qur'an was written against Catholicism and the idea of trinity rather than for religious truth. Some examples:

---

6   Qur'an, 8:65
7   Qur'an, 4:91
8   Qur'an, 5:33,35
9   Qur'an, 66:9
10   Qur'an, 48:29
11   Qur'an, 4:47

- Unbelievers are those who say: "Allah is the Messiah [Jesus], son of Mary."[12]

- Those who say that Allah is the Messiah, son of Mary, are unbelievers. Unbelievers too are those who said that Allah is a third of three [the trinity].[13]

- You shall find the most hostile people to the believers to be the Jews and the polytheists.[14]

- O believers, do not take the Jews and the Christians as friends; some of them are friends of each other. Whoever of you takes them as friends is surely one of them. Allah indeed does not guide the wrongdoers.[15]

- Allah said: "O Jesus, son of Mary, did you say to the people: 'Take me and my mother as gods, apart from Allah?'"[16]

- O People of the Book, do not exceed the bounds of your religion, nor say about Allah except the truth. The Messiah, Jesus, son of Mary, is only Allah's Messenger and His word, which He imparted to Mary, and is a spirit from Him! So believe in Allah and His Messengers and do not say "three" (gods).[17]

- There is a group of them who twist their tongues while reading the Book, so that you may suppose it is a part of the Book; whereas it is not a part of the Book. They also say: "It is from Allah," whereas it is not from Allah.[18]

---

12   Qur'an, 5:17
13   Qur'an, 5:72,74
14   Qur'an, 5:82
15   Qur'an, 5:51
16   Qur'an, 5:116
17   Qur'an, 4:171
18   Qur'an, 3:78

- Woe unto those who write the Book with their hands, then say it is from Allah in order to sell it for a small price.[19]

One of the reasons the West will not see a decline in the terrorists' furor, manifested in such activities as suicide bombings, is because of the reward Allah promises his followers if they die while fighting for Islam. Here are two examples:

- Allah has bought from the believers their lives and their wealth in return for Paradise; they fight in the Way of Allah, kill and get killed.[20]

- Whoever fights in the Way of Allah and is killed or conquers, We shall accord him a great reward.[21]

Our values and freedoms are being, and will be, challenged if "hate speech" or "blasphemy against religion" laws are instituted in the United Nations and supported by Western countries. The institution of such laws that forbid free speech about religion into the United Nations, will not cure the terrorists' furor. If the Qur'an became subject to these laws, these laws would only infuriate the terrorist even more, considering that Muslims are taught that Islam supersedes every other religion. Here are two examples that teach the Muslim that the Qur'an surpasses any other religion:

- And We have revealed to you the Book in truth, confirming the scriptures that preceded it and superceding [sic] it.[22]

- It is He Who sent forth His Messenger with guidance and the religion of truth, that He may exalt it above every other religion.[23]

The United Nations is occupied by many Muslim nations; will it be time for the West to leave the United Nations?

---

19   Qur'an, 2:79
20   Qur'an, 9:111
21   Qur'an, 4:74
22   Qur'an, 5:48
23   Qur'an, 48:28

One need only to look at the statistics offered by those who have followed the spread of Islam into the rest of the world in order to recognize that we must proceed with educated caution (*Slavery, Terrorism, & Islam: The Historical Roots and Contemporary Threat* by Dr. Peter Hammond).[24]

Only after reading the Qur'an and recognizing its influence over Muslims, can the Western world comprehend that it is engaging in negotiations with a religious ideology that is driven to domination, not peaceful co-existence. The "Christian" West will never stop Islamic terrorism with compromising negotiations. All Muslims are led by the dictates of Muhammad, written in the Qur'an, in which he told them that it (the Qur'an) is the word of God; but some become fanatical about it.

For any Muslim, no matter the sect, the Qur'an/Koran is revered as holy. Any words, ideas, or actions that are contrary to the Qur'an and its messenger/teacher, Muhammad, are considered denigrating, disrespectful, and offensive. Therefore, to the radical follower of the Qur'an, the very idea of free speech and democracy (a government by the people) opposes a government by Islamic Sharia law; it contradicts the very foundation of Islamic thought, and it is considered blasphemy.

Today, as never before, because of the terrorist's willingness to use weapons of mass destruction, it is absolutely necessary to bring about a proper understanding of differing religions; there is a need for each religious group to examine not only the beliefs of others, but also their own beliefs.

Troubling times are ahead of us, the United Nations and our governments need to be informed of what the Qur'an is. The sooner the truth is acted upon, the less deaths there will be.

I am not Islamophobic, I do not fear Muslims, nor do I hate them; actually I feel sorry for them. I simply recognize that they have been bound to a belief system that forces them to hate non-Muslims.

24 Dr. Peter Hammond, Slavery, Terrorism and Islam, The Historical Roots and Contemporary Threat, Published by Xulon Press, ISBN - 9781612154985

Neither am I racist; Muslims come in a variety of colors, cultures, and countries. Islam is not a race, it is an ideology. They need to look outside their religion so that they can properly see their own religion.

If a Christian or Jew was to claim blasphemy against a Muslim, he would have plenty of examples to choose from. The following is just a few paraphrased selections from the Qur'an that Christians would consider to be lies because of the Bible:

- Christians and Jews transformed into monkeys and swine (chapter 5 vs.59,60).

- Christians and Jews are transgressors (chapter 5 vs.59).

- Jesus made from dirt (chapter 3 vs.59).

- Jesus supposedly predicting some future messenger named Ahmad (chapter 61 vs.6)

...the list goes on.

The United Nations has received requests from several Islamic dominated countries to institute blasphemy laws. Canada, being one of those nations, already has blasphemy laws, although seldom used. The Canadian Criminal Code states:

Section 296

(1) Everyone who publishes a blasphemous libel is guilty of an indictable offense and liable to imprisonment for a term not exceeding two years.

Section 318

(1) Every one who advocates or promotes genocide is guilty of an indictable offense and liable to imprisonment for a term not exceeding five years.

(2) In this section, "genocide" means any of the following acts committed with intent to destroy in whole or in part any identifiable group, namely,

(a) killing members of the group; or

(b) deliberately inflicting on the group conditions of life calculated to bring about its physical destruction.

(4) In this section, "identifiable group" means any section of the public distinguished by color, race, religion, ethnic origin or sexual orientation.

Section 319

(1) Every one who, by communicating statements in any public place, incites hatred against any identifiable group where such incitement is likely to lead to a breach of the peace is guilty of

(a) an indictable offense and is liable to imprisonment for a term not exceeding two years; or

(b) an offense punishable on summary conviction.

(2) Every one who, by communicating statements, other than in private conversation, willfully promotes hatred against any identifiable group is guilty of

(a) an indictable offense and is liable to imprisonment for a term not exceeding two years; or

(b) an offense punishable on summary conviction.

According to the Canadian Criminal Code, the Qur'an should be labeled hate propaganda now. Why is it that in Canada the Qur'an has not been subject to these laws already?

If the Canadian Constitution's Charter of Rights and Freedoms states *Whereas Canada is founded upon principles that recognize the supremacy of God and the rule of law*, then Canadians should recognize God's supremacy. If God is supreme, then God's laws should take precedence over man's laws. But which religion tells the truth about God?

Muhammad, who was illiterate, spoke of himself as being "a messenger of God" equal to the Bible's Abraham, Moses, and Jesus. He claims that the Qur'an supersedes the holy books of the Jews and Christians because their books have been "corrupted". Therefore, Muslims are taught not to read the books of Jews and Christians.

Who is Moses and what did he teach? Who is Jesus and what did He teach? Who is Muhammad and what did he teach?

The first one teaches us to love God and to love our neighbor; the second one teaches us to love God, to love our neighbor, and to love our enemy; the third one, Muhammad, teaches his followers to kill those who don't obey Muhammad.

By what authority do each of these historical figures teach? That question should be resolved by the end of this book.

Knowing what we know about the Qur'an with its instructions to dominate, how will we in the West be prepared to deal with growing terrorism? Do we have the will to take the necessary steps to cure the problem? Bringing an end to terrorism starts by changing the mindset of the terrorist: he needs help. If the Qur'an is his only source for the knowledge of God, his knowledge is superficial. We all need a better understanding of religious differences so that we can help the terrorist change his ways.

CHAPTER 2 - THE CURE

The cure is education; knowing the truth, and properly understanding religious differences. Unfortunately, the truth has been obscured by the chaos that the originators of the Roman Catholic Church created. Each of the three major monotheistic religions – Judaism, Christianity and Islam – believes that it alone is representing the truth about God to the world; each group states that "God is one." In the Jewish Torah and the Christian Bible, Moses wrote:

→ Hear, O Israel: The Lord our God, the Lord is one.[25]

And when Jesus was asked what the most important commandment was, He prefaced it with the same statement. Jesus said:

25   Bible, New International Version, The Zondervan Corporation, copyright 1978, Deuteronomy chapter 6 vs. 4

→ "The most important one is this: 'Hear, O Israel, the Lord our God, the Lord is one.'"[26]

Only then did He state the command:

→ "Love the Lord your God with all your heart and with all your soul and with all your mind and all your strength."[27]

He immediately added these words:

→ "The second is this: 'Love your neighbor as yourself.' There is no commandment greater than these."[28]

However, at the first Council of Constantinople in 381 A.D., in order to combat many religious theories of the day (modalism, monarchianism, Arianism, Sabellianism, etc.) the Church (by this time the Church was under the control of the Roman Empire – the beginning of the Roman Catholic Church), modified the doctrinal statements made in 325 A.D., at the First Council of Nicaea. The Church removed the statement "The Son is the essence of the Father" and added the statement "The Holy Ghost [Spirit] is to worshiped together with the Father and the Son" thus giving the concept of "three persons of the trinity of God" – three in one. The Church surmised that these three titles of God constituted three persons, and this doctrine of the trinity is still believed and taught by most Christians today. Any Christian who does not believe in this trinity is accused of "modalism." This book is not modalistic.

It is necessary for some dictionary definitions here:

• Mode – *a manner or form of being.*

• Being – *a living thing, existence, as opposed to nonexistence* [God is the Supreme Being].

• Individual – *existing as a unit; single, a person.*

---

26 Bible, Mark 12:29

27 Bible, Mark 12:30

28 Bible, Mark 12:31

- Person – *any human being considered as a distinct entity or personality; an individual.*

The dictionary, influenced by religion, also gives these definitions:

- Person – *one of the three individualities in the trinity.*

- Modalism – *The theological doctrine that the members of the trinity are not three distinct persons but rather three modes of forms of activity (the Father, Son, and Holy Spirit) under which God manifests himself.*

The definition for modalism is itself confusing. If the word *mode* means a *being*, and a *person* is a *being*, then the definition given here of modalism is stating that the "members of the trinity" are not three beings but that they are three beings (modes). This makes no sense. Using the words *three modes of forms of activity*, or *three beings of forms of activity*, makes no sense either. If the concept of modalism is that God changes from one form to another, then that is impossible, for God is immutable.

Biblical scriptures will be used in the first chapter of Part 2 to explain the reason that both Moses and Jesus were emphatic in their statements that "the Lord is one."

The chaos the "trinity" created has brought more division in Christian Churches than any other issue. Muslim, Catholic, Christian, Jehovah's Witness, Mormon, or Jew…they all have their roots in the Bible, or portions of it. The main difference in all six of these religions is based upon what they believe about Jesus and what He taught. The Muslim believes Jesus to be a prophet, not God, nor the son of God; the Catholic and the Christian believe him to be the son of God; the Jehovah's Witness believes him to be another god; the Mormon believes that he is one of many gods, and the Jew rejects him completely. But if all of these religious groups sat down together to compare books – not theories, nor doctrines, but books – it would not take long to settle their differences.

PART 2 - THE BIBLE VS. THE QUR'AN

CHAPTER 1- THE BIBLE

(The Bible quotations are taken from
the New International Version)

Christianity started before Jesus, the Christ, was incarnated; indeed, much more than two thousand years ago. *Christ*, from which we get our word *Christian*, comes from the Greek word *Christos*, which translates the Hebrew word *Messiah*. Christ/Messiah is not a name, but rather a title. (Messiah: *the Anointed One, a deliverer and ruler of Israel promised by God and expected by the Jews.*)

The Messiah's coming was predicted long ago in Hebrew Scriptures by: Moses in 1420 B.C., King David in 990 B.C., Isaiah in 760 B.C., Zechariah in 520 B.C., and Malachi in 400 B.C. (dates approximate). The Bible states that Jesus is the Christ, and Christians follow His teachings. Although Jews do not accept Jesus as their Messiah, both the Bible and the Qur'an state that Jesus is the Messiah (Qur'an).[29]

Who is Jesus and by what authority does he teach? (This same question will be explored in chapter three of Muhammad's authority, from verses found in the Qur'an).

Christians call the man Jesus by many names: Lord, God, Son of God, Savior, and so on...but no man can become God, so why do they call him this?

The Bible states that Jesus was much more than a prophet or the "son of God." Jesus' apostle John wrote:

→ In the beginning was the Word, and the Word was with God, and the Word was God.[30]

The term *Word* is the English translation of the Greek word *Logos* (the original form of the New Testament portion of the Bible that we have today, was written in Greek), and a dictionary meaning for this word is: *cosmic reason giving order, purpose, and intelligibility to the world.* In other words, Divine Expression – God speaking. Jesus' apostle John also tells us:

→ The Word became flesh and lived for a while among us.[31]

Jesus' apostle Paul wrote:

→ In Christ all the fullness of the Deity lives in bodily form.[32]

→ The Son is the radiance of God's glory and the exact representation of His being.[33]

---

29   Qur'an, 4:171
30   Bible, John 1:1
31   Bible, John 1:14
32   Bible, Colossians 2:9
33   Bible, Hebrews 1:3

Not a man becoming God, but God manifesting Himself as a man.

The Bible states that Jesus spoke in parables:

> → Jesus spoke all these things in parables; he did not say anything to them without using a parable.[34]

Jesus stated:

> → I have much more to say to you, more than you can now bear. Though I have been speaking figuratively, a time is coming when I will no longer use this kind of language but will tell you plainly about my Father.[35]

Jesus, even though he spoke of himself as a man, was a living parable; He was God in flesh. God did not want man to think of God as a fleshly being, but to know Him as He is – Spirit.

> → God is Spirit, and his worshipers must worship in spirit and in truth.[36]

God, after sending many prophets throughout many centuries to teach us, finally manifested Himself, as an example of how a man should live, and, more importantly, to demonstrate His love for mankind. As a man, He died on the cross to pay for our sins; because He is God, He rose from the dead.

Christians who believe that God is three persons – a trinity (Father, Son, and Holy Spirit) – have not compared the verses that show God and Jesus to be the same person.

The following seven subtitles will have comparable verses from scripture to show that Yahweh/Jehovah God revealed Himself as the man Jesus. (Some Christians render the Hebrew word YHWH as *Jehovah*

---

34   Bible, Matthew 13:34
35   Bible, John 16:12,25
36   Bible, John 4:24

and others render it *Yahweh*. The English letter J did not come into existence until the fourteenth century.)

1. I am (Yahweh / Jehovah) Jesus

The word or name Yahweh in Hebrew means: *I am*. It is recorded in the Bible that Moses asked God for His name, God replied:

> → I am who I am.[37]

The name Jesus comes to us from the Greek *Iesous,* which is borrowed from the Hebrew word *Yeshuä* (Greek does not have the letters j, sh, or ä), and this Hebrew name means *Yah – saves.* Yah is a contraction for *Yahweh,* found in Psalm 68:4, in the King James Version of the Bible. The name Jesus, contains the name Yahweh plus the word saves – Yah-saves. If you prefer the word Jehovah rather than Yahweh, then here is another way to see it:

Jehoshua / Joshua = Jehovah-saved;

Jeshua = Jah-saves (Hebrew) = Iesous (Greek) = Jesus (English).

Jesus equates Himself with God:

> → I tell you the truth, before Abraham was born, I am.[38]

Abraham lived many years before Jesus entered the world.

> → Call his name Jesus, for he will save his people from their sins.[39]

2. One Lord

Both Yahweh of the Old Testament and Jesus of the New Testament are called *Lord*, yet the Bible states that there is only one Lord. (The

---

37   Bible, Exodus 3:14

38   Bible, John 8:58

39   Bible, Matthew 1:21

word *Lord* when capitalized *LORD* in our English translations of the Old Testament originally was written *Yahweh*, not Lord.)

Examples:

→ This is what the Sovereign LORD [Yahweh] says:...[40]

→ There is one body and one Spirit...one Lord, one faith, one baptism; one God and Father of all...[41]

→ God has made this Jesus, whom you crucified, both Lord and Christ.[42]

3. Savior

In the Old Testament, Yahweh says that He is the only God and the only Savior, yet the Bible calls Jesus God and Savior.

Examples:

→ Before me no God was formed, nor will there be one after me. I am the Lord [Yahweh] and apart from me there is no savior.[43]

→ I the LORD [Yahweh], am your Savior, your Redeemer, the Mighty One of Jacob.[44]

→ We wait for the blessed hope, the glorious appearing of our great God and Savior, Jesus Christ.[45]

4. Redeemer, King of Israel, First and Last

---

40 Bible, Isaiah 65:13
41 Bible, Ephesians 4:4,5,6
42 Bible, Acts 2:36
43 Bible, Isaiah 43:10
44 Bible, Isaiah 49:26
45 Bible, Titus 2:13

Yahweh is called Redeemer, the First and the Last, and King of Israel. Jesus bears these same titles.

Examples:

→ This is what the LORD [Yahweh] says – Israel's *King* and *Redeemer*, the LORD [Yahweh] Almighty: I am the *first* and I am the *last*; apart from me there is no God.[46]

→ Christ *redeemed* us from the curse of the law by becoming a curse for us.[47]

→ Nathanael declared, "Rabbi, you are the Son of God; the *King* of Israel." Jesus said: "You believe…"[48]

→ I am the *First* and the *Last*, I am the living one; I was dead, and behold I am alive forever.[49]

We know this was Jesus speaking in Revelation 1:18 because He said: "I was dead," the physical man, or flesh, not the Spirit.

5. Father

Isaiah said Yahweh is our Father, and he called Jesus "Everlasting Father," yet Jesus said there is only one Father in heaven.

Examples:

→ You, O Lord [Yahweh], are our Father, our Redeemer from old is your name.[50]

---

46   Bible, Isaiah 44:6
47   Bible, Galatians 3:13
48   Bible, John 1:49,50
49   Bible, Revelation 1:18
50   Bible, Isaiah 63:16

→ For to us a child is born, to us a son is given, and the government will be on his shoulders. And he will be called Wonderful Counselor, Mighty God, Everlasting Father, Prince of Peace.[51]

Jesus said:

→ You are not to be called "Rabbi," for you have only one Master and you are all brothers. And do not call anyone on earth "father," for you have one Father, and he is in heaven. Nor are you to be called "teacher," for you have one Teacher, the Christ.[52]

→ This is how you should pray: "Our Father in heaven…"[53]

Even those who followed Jesus had a hard time understanding who the man Jesus really was:

→ Philip said to him, "Lord, show us the Father, and that will be enough for us." Jesus answered, "Don't you know me, Philip, even after I have been among you such a long time? Anyone who has seen me has seen the Father."[54]

Seeing the Spirit, not the flesh.

6. The Counselor

Jesus' apostle John, in writing his Gospel, either contradicted himself or wrote the truth when he penned the verses in the Gospel of John, chapters 14 and 16. In chapter 14, verse 16 and verse 26, Jesus says the Father will send the Counselor, but in chapter 16 verse 7, Jesus says that He (Jesus) will send the Counselor (Holy Spirit). Previously, in Isaiah 9:6, Isaiah calls Jesus, *Counselor*. This only makes sense knowing God as being one, not three in one.

Examples:

---

51 Bible, Isaiah 9:6
52 Bible, Matthew 23:8,9,10
53 Bible, Matthew 6:9
54 Bible, John 14:8,9

→ I will ask the Father, and He will give you another Counselor to be with you forever, the Spirit of truth.[55]

→ The Counselor, the Holy Spirit, whom the Father will send in my name, will teach you all things and will remind you of everything I have said to you.[56]

→ I tell you the truth: It is for your good that I am going away. Unless I go away, the Counselor will not come to you; but if I go, I will send Him to you.[57]

→ For to us a child is born, to us a son [Jesus] is given, and the government will be on his shoulders. And he will be called Wonderful Counselor, Mighty God, Everlasting Father, Prince of Peace.[58]

Jesus called the Counselor "the Spirit of truth," and Jesus called Himself the truth.

→ I am the way the truth and the life. No one comes to the Father except through me. If you really knew me, you would know my Father as well. From now on, you do know Him and have seen Him.[59]

7. The Spirit

Jesus, speaking as a man, said the following:

→ If anyone loves me, he will obey my teaching. My Father will love him, and we will come to him and make our home with him.[60]

---

55   Bible, John 14:16
56   Bible, John 14:26
57   Bible, John 16:7
58   Bible, Isaiah 9:6
59   Bible, John 14:6,7
60   Bible, John 14:23

> → Whoever has my commands and obeys them, he is the one who loves me. He who loves me, will be loved by my Father, and I too will love him and show myself to him.[61]

Jesus shows Himself when He comes to live in us as the Holy Spirit.

> → God is Spirit and His worshipers must worship in spirit and truth.[62]

Jesus' apostle Paul said:

> → Don't you know that you yourselves are God's temple and that God's Spirit lives in you?[63]

(That is, if you are "born again.")

> → Now the Lord is the Spirit [Jesus is Lord] and, where the Spirit of the Lord is, there is freedom. The Lord is the Spirit.[64]

> → In Christ all the fullness of the Deity lives in bodily form.[65]

Jesus called Himself the truth:

> → Jesus answered, "I am the way and the truth and the life."[66]

Then, two chapters later, Jesus speaks of Himself in the third person:

> → But when He, the Spirit of truth comes, He will guide you into all truth. He will not speak on his own, He will speak only what He hears and He will tell you what is yet to come.[67]

---

61   Bible, John 14:21
62   Bible, John 4:24
63   Bible, 1 Corinthians 3:16
64   Bible, 2 Corinthians 3:17,18
65   Bible, Colossians 2: 9
66   Bible, John 14:6
67   Bible, John 16:13

When we realize that Jesus is the Holy Spirit, then we can better understand why He said these next three verses:

→ The world cannot accept Him, because it neither sees Him nor knows Him. But you know Him, for He lives with you and will be in you. I will not leave you as orphans; I will come to you. Before long, the world will not see me anymore, but you will see me.[68]

While this may sound confusing, there is a good reason; look at what Paul states in the following verses:

→ No one knows the thoughts of God except the Spirit of God. We have not received the spirit of the world, but the Spirit who is from God, that we may understand what God has freely given us. This is what we speak, not in words taught us by human wisdom, but in words taught by the Spirit, expressing spiritual truths in spiritual words. The man without the Spirit does not accept the things that come from the Spirit of God, for they are foolishness to him, and he cannot understand them, because they are spiritually discerned.[69]

→ To this day the same veil remains when the old covenant [the Old Testament or Torah] is read. It has not been removed, because only in Christ is it taken away. Even to this day when Moses [the Torah] is read, a veil covers their hearts. But whenever anyone turns to the Lord [Jesus], the veil is taken away. Now the Lord is the Spirit, and where the Spirit of the Lord is, there is freedom.[70]

From these verses about the Spirit we can understand how a non-Christian has difficulty understanding; however, equally so the Christian of today may not understand because of the traditional teaching of the Church to which he or she has been conditioned. Paul also equates the words Christ and God when he says:

---

68 Bible, John 14:17,18,19
69 Bible, 1 Corinthians 2:11,12,13,14
70 Bible, 2 Corinthians 3:14,15,16,17

→ You, however, are controlled not by the sinful nature but by the Spirit, if the *Spirit of God* lives in you. And if anyone does not have the *Spirit of Christ*, he does not belong to Christ.[71]

If we accept Jesus as our Lord, then we can ask Him for His gift of His Spirit.

There is only one Spirit. God is the Holy Spirit, the word *Holy* is an adjective modifying the noun *Spirit*.

→ God is Spirit.[72]

Jesus is the Holy Spirit:

→ Now the Lord is the Spirit.[73]

There is only one Spirit:

→ There is one body and one Spirit...[74]

God is the Word:

→ In the beginning was the Word, and the Word was with God, and the Word was God.[75]

God, the Word, became the man Jesus:

→ The Word became flesh and lived for a while among us.

---

71   Bible, Romans 8:9
72   Bible, John 4:24
73   Bible, 2 Corinthians 3:17
74   Bible, Ephesians 4:4
75   Bible, John 1:1

Summary of Chapter 1

Why did God, our Father Creator, who is Spirit, present Himself as the "Son" of God? One answer is that God did not want man to form an image in his mind of God, who is infinite and omnipresent, as a finite, three-dimensional (height/width/depth) person of flesh and bone. When Jesus came in the flesh as the Son of God, He spoke and lived as an example of a man in perfect obedience to our Father Creator – sinless, and, to show His great love, He died on the cross to pay for our sins.

The meaning given for the word *spirit* in both Hebrew and Greek from Strong's Concordance[76] is the idea of air moving – a current of air or a breath of air. Although no material substance such as air will ever describe spirit, it is the closest thing we have. If we were to think of air as being omnipresent as God is omnipresent, and to think of that air taking on moisture as God took on flesh, we would have the nearest comparison that we could think of to describe spirit. Just as we cannot see air which is all around us – ever-present, we cannot see God who is omnipresent – ever-present; but when air takes on moisture as God took on flesh, we see a cloud within that ever present air. It has the appearance of height/width/depth, similar to God, Who took on flesh as a man, appearing as the man Jesus.

Jesus often spoke in parables, and as a man, was a living parable. He was God, who is Spirit, within a flesh and bone body, speaking to us – Divine Expression.

→ The Son is the radiance of God's glory and the exact representation of His being.[77]

Not the physical formation of flesh, but the person within the body, because God is not flesh and bone, He is Spirit.

---

76 *Strong's Exhaustive Concordance of the Bible*, Thomas Nelson Publishers, 1984 ISBN - 0-8407-5360-8

77 Bible, Hebrews 1:3

Jesus – who is Spirit – is God. Because He is God, nothing is impossible; He can do anything. When He died on the cross, He died a physical death, and because He is God, He rose from the dead. Jesus called Himself the resurrection:

→ I am the resurrection and the life.[78]

→ Nothing is impossible with God.[79]

→ In Christ all the fullness of the Deity lives in bodily form.[80]

Jesus said:

→ I and the Father are one.[81]

(That is, one and the same.)

God, our loving Father, came to us in human form, giving His human life to pay for our sins. The Bible states:

→ The Word became flesh and lived for a while among us.[82]

Jesus as man was called *Emmanuel*, which means *God with us*.[83]

When God spoke to Moses at the burning bush (Exodus 3:4), He spoke as our Father Creator from heaven. When we call on the Lord Jesus (Yah-saves), Jesus, our Father in heaven, who is Spirit comes to live in us as the Holy Spirit. He now speaks to us as the Holy Spirit inside of us *if* we are *born again* (also called "baptized in the Spirit").

Three verses from the Bible, Matthew 3:11, Mark 1:8, and Luke 3:16, all state:

---

78   Bible, John 11:25
79   Bible, Luke 1:37
80   Bible, Colossians 2:9
81   Bible, John 10:30
82   Bible, John 1:14
83   Bible, Matthew 1:23

→ He [Jesus] will baptize you with the Holy Spirit and fire.

The first part of 1 John 2:27 states:

→ The anointing [Holy Spirit] you received from Him remains in you, and you do not need anyone to teach you.

The Bible was not meant to be interpreted by man; its spiritual meanings are revealed by the Holy Spirit – Jesus. When we read the Bible, we need to ask the Lord Jesus to help us to understand it.

→ If any of you lacks wisdom, he should ask God, who gives generously to all without finding fault, and it will be given to him.[84]

Jesus said:

→ You may ask me for anything in my name, and I will do it.[85]

This chapter has presented the unity or oneness of God. God Himself took on flesh as the man Jesus. Jesus is God. In contrast, the next chapter will give some examples of the teaching doctrine of the three persons in one, or trinity, found in most churches today.

---

84   Bible, James 1:5
85   Bible, John 14:14

CHAPTER 2 - EXAMINING THE TRINITARIAN DOCTRINE

Shortly after writing the previous chapter, I took it to a professor of theology who, after reading it, gave me sixty-six pages he photo-copied from six different theological books that supported the trinity concept. After studying them I wrote this next chapter and returned to him for his comments. His words were: "In my twenty years of teaching, no student has done what you have done." Speaking of the authors of these six books he then said: "At best, they muddy the waters." He knew these books were not good but still taught his students from them.

For clarity, here again are some definitions of words used in this chapter, taken from the *Funk and Wagnalls Standard College Dictionary*, 1989 edition:

- Being – *a living thing, existence, as opposed to nonexistence.*

- Coequal – *the equal of another or others.*

- Distinct – *recognizably not the same; clearly different.*

- Essence – *an existent being; especially, an immaterial being – spirit.*

- Individual – *existing as a unit; single, a person.*

- Person – *any human being* [God is the Supreme Being] *considered as a distinct entity or personality; an individual.*

The dictionary, influenced by religion, also gives this definition for person: *one of the three individualities in the Trinity.*

The following excerpts are from the books the professor showed me, with my comments.

1. *Introductory Lectures in Systematic Theology*[86]

From chapter nine Thiessen states:

- I The Unity of God: There can be only one infinite and perfect being. That the divine nature is undivided and indivisible is intimated in Deut. 6:4: "Hear, O Israel: Jehovah our God is one Jehovah." That is, God does not consist of parts nor can He be divided into parts. His being is simple; man's is compound, having both a material and an immaterial part. But God is spirit and is not susceptible of such division.

Here we can see that Thiessen has correctly stated that God is one. But then, he contradicts himself by stating the following:

- II The Trinity of God: By the Trinity we mean that there are three eternal distinctions in the one divine essence, known respectively

86   Henry Clarence Thiessen, *Introductory Lectures in Systematic Theology*, Publisher Wm. B. Eerdmans, 2006, ISBN - 978-0-8028-2729-6

as Father, Son, and Holy Spirit. These three distinctions are three persons, and so we may speak of the tripersonality of God. The three are equal.

Here, we have been told that these three persons of the "trinity" are coequal, equal in power. If the Son was equal to the Father, then the Son would have had equal authority to send the Father. But, in truth, a son is subordinate to his father.

If we have three distinct persons or individual beings, we have three living things or existences. This means tritheism, three gods.

If the word essence means an existent being – spirit, how can the Holy Spirit be "in the one divine essence," a spirit within a spirit? God is one.

Jesus said:

→ God is spirit, and his worshipers must worship in spirit and truth.[87]

Jesus' apostle Paul wrote:

→ Now the Lord [Jesus] is the Spirit.[88]

Philip (a disciple of Jesus) said to Him:

→ Lord, show us the Father, and that will be enough for us.[89]

Jesus answers Philip with this statement:

→ Don't you know me Philip, even after I have been among you such a long time? Anyone who has seen me has seen the Father.[90]

---

87   Bible, John 4:24

88   Bible, 2 Corinthians 3:17

89   Bible, John 14:8

90   Bible, John 14:9

Jesus was speaking of seeing the Spirit or person within the body, not the body itself. God our Father is Spirit, a Holy Spirit, He was in a fleshly body as the Son, and now lives in us as the Holy Spirit.

Jesus' apostle Paul equates the *Spirit of God* and the *Spirit of Christ* as being one and the same:

→ You, however, are controlled not by the sinful nature but by the Spirit, if the Spirit of God lives in you. And if anyone does not have the Spirit of Christ, he does not belong to Christ.[91]

A.W. Tozer, in his book *Knowledge of the Holy*,[92] wrote:

• "We might be wise to follow the insight of the enraptured heart rather than the more cautious reasonings of the theological mind."[93]

It is only when we are conscious of spirit that we *see* what God is – Spirit.

2. Introducing Christian Doctrine[94]

In his book, Millard J. Erickson titles his 11th chapter "God's Three-in-Oneness: The Trinity."

The Bible states:

→ So God created man in his own image, in the image of God he created him; male and female he created them.[95]

The statement from the Bible, "God created man in His own image" has so often been misunderstood by being thought of in reverse. The

91   Bible, Romans 8:9

92   A.W. Tozer, *Knowledge of the Holy*, Harper Collins Publishers, copyright 1961, ISBN - 0060684127

93   *Knowledge of the Holy*, chapter 3, 5th paragraph

94   Millard J. Erickson, *Introducing Christian Doctrine*, Publisher Baker Academic, 2001, ISBN - 0801022509

95   Bible, Genesis 1:27

following statements by Erickson show that he is thinking of God in man's image, not man in God's image.

- The image of God in man is to be found in the fact that man has been created male and female. This means that the image of God must consist in a unity in plurality.[96]

God is Spirit. Man, better understood as mankind, was created in God's image, therefore man is a spiritual being in a fleshly body. Mankind can be found in either a male or a female body.

Mr. Erickson wrote:

- God – He is an organism, that is, a unity of distinct parts.[97]

God has no parts. When Jesus and Moses taught the most important commandment – the first commandment – they both prefaced it with this statement:

→ Hear O Israel, the Lord our God, the Lord is one.[98]

This next statement reveals why we have so many variations of Christian doctrine.

- Although the doctrine of the Trinity is not expressly asserted, the Scripture, particularly the New Testament, contains so many suggestions of the deity and unity of the three persons that we can understand why the church formulated the doctrine, and concluded that they were right in doing so.[99]

The church should never formulate doctrine. Believing in the Bible just as it is written, whether we understand it or not, is superior to forming a doctrine of what we don't fully understand. Because the church did not understand, it created its own interpretation.

---

96   *Introducing Christian Doctrine*, page 100
97   *Introducing Christian Doctrine*, page 100
98   Bible, Mark 12:29, Deuteronomy 6:4
99   *Introducing Christian Doctrine*, page 100

The original error of creating the doctrine of the trinity was itself created by thinking that three terms or names for God constituted three persons, rather than believing that God, our Father Creator, became flesh as the Son, and is now in us as the Holy Spirit. Jesus said that if we obeyed His commands that He would show Himself to us – the Holy Spirit (John 14:21). God is one and is Spirit, Jesus said:

→ I and the Father are one.[100]

God is not composed of three persons. When God as the man Jesus prayed to God as Father, He was being an example for us. Nothing is impossible for God to do; after all, Christians do accept John 1:1:

→ …the Word was with God, and the Word was God.

Under his subtitle "The Orthodox Formulation" Erickson explains how, at the Council of Constantine (381 A.D.), the orthodox doctrine of the trinity was enunciated to combat other doctrines, monarchianism, modalism, and the like.[101] He previously admits:

- In modalistic monarchianism we have a genuinely unique, original, and creative conception, and one which is in some ways a brilliant breakthrough.[102]

The only problem with modalistic monarchianism is the limited human conception – thinking that God can only be in one "mode" at a time. But for God nothing is impossible. If Trinitarians can believe that God is somehow three persons in one person, why is it so difficult for them to believe that God, who is one, couldn't reveal Himself three different ways at the same time? One revealed three ways; not three components joined as one. (A man can be a father to his children, a son to his parents, and a husband to his wife, all at the same time; he is still one man. He *relates* in three differing ways.)

---

100   Bible, John 10:30
101   *Introducing Christian Doctrine*, page 102
102   *Introducing Christian Doctrine*, page 101

Nothing is impossible for God. God is Spirit, and we must think of spirit when we speak of God. He is infinite. If He, Who tells us that He is one, so chooses to reveal Himself three ways at one time, who are we to debate what He is?

If we are to conclude that God must be three in one, a trinity, because we saw Him in the man Jesus praying to the Father, then we must conclude that God is not just a triune God, but a multi-God. Why, because He is in many Christians. The Holy Spirit, who is God, lives in "baptized in the Spirit" Christians. Does this divide Him? What if God had revealed Himself in two men, or a man and a woman, would He then be Quadripartite rather than Triune?

If God is a trinity, then when Jesus walked as a man, could not the Father have also visited us as a man at the same time? (Sounds like Mormonism; more on this later.)

God is Spirit, and we must look at Him in the spirit to understand Spirit. God, who is Spirit, is infinitely one, never parts. God our Father whom we cannot see, revealed Himself in a flesh-and-bone body to show His love for us, and now lives in us. He is Spirit and He is Holy, He is the Holy Spirit. The word *Holy* is an adjective, a descriptive word modifying the noun *Spirit*.

To be saved we have been given only one name by which to call Him – Jesus (Yah-saves, Yahweh-saves). God Himself came to save us. He now lives in us.

God is Spirit (John 4:24); our Father is Spirit (Matthew 10:20); Jesus is Spirit (2 Corinthians 3:17)

→ There is one body and one Spirit...one Lord...one God and Father.[103]

To call the Holy Spirit as someone beside Jesus or beside the Father is to say that we have three Spirits for our God – a tritheistic concept.

---

103 Bible, Ephesians 4:4,5,6

Both Moses and Jesus had good reason to preface the first commandment with the statement:

→ Hear, O Israel: The Lord our God is one.

The problem some people develop for themselves in thinking that if Jesus and the Father are one, and therefore God must have died on the cross, and that would be impossible, is that they cannot believe God for what seems impossible to man. Jesus said:

→ I am the resurrection.[104]

It was the flesh that died, not the person. We know the Word has always existed and is God, who cannot die. This is what the Lord [Yahweh] says:

→ I am the First and I am the Last; apart from me there is no God.[105]

But one has to contend with Jesus' statement:

→ I am the First and the Last. I am the living one; I was dead, and behold I am alive forever.[106]

Praise God that we simple human beings do not need to understand everything to know God; we just need to trust Him, to believe Him.

→ Without faith it is impossible to please God.[107]

If God were three persons, then Matthew 28:19 would be incorrect:

→ ...baptizing them in the name of the Father and of the Son and of the Holy Spirit.

---

104 Bible, John 11:25
105 Bible, Isaiah 44:6
106 Bible, Revelation 1:18
107 Bible, Hebrews 11:16

Three persons would have three names. The word *name* in this verse is singular for good reason.

From the Old Testament, God was called Yahweh, the name Jesus means Yahweh-saves. God is Spirit, the Holy Spirit. The Holy Spirit is what God is, not a name.

The Bible specifically states that this name Jesus is the only name by which we must be saved. Why? Because Yahweh, who is Spirit, took on flesh and died on the cross for us paying for our sins: Yah-saves = Jesus.

> → The Son is the radiance of God's glory and the exact representation of His being.[108]

Man cannot see God with his eyes; God is Spirit, but He became flesh for us. When we call God Jesus, we are acknowledging His payment for our sins. The only name I should call God my Father is Jesus (Yahweh-saves); the only name I should call the Spirit inside me is Jesus (God is Spirit, the Lord is Spirit); the one who died for me is Jesus. When we look at Jesus we need to see, not the flesh which can be seen and touched, but the heart or spirit of Him, that is who He is. God is Spirit, not flesh and blood. God lived in a body; He was not *the* body. John 1:14 states: "The Word became flesh."

We Christians are thinking of God in human terms; we need to spend time in prayer, that is, praising and thanking Him for who He is as Spirit. He then will reveal more of Himself to us, and then we will understand Spirit.

On page 103 of Mr. Erickson's book, under the subtitle of "Essential Elements of a Doctrine of the Trinity," he writes:

• The unity of God may be compared to the unity of husband and wife.

Here again we have a man thinking of God in man's image. God has been and will always be one, infinitely. A man and a woman are united

---

108   Bible, Hebrews 1:3

in marriage, not in body, they are companions. At one time they were separate. This statement of Erickson's does not stand up. On the next page (104), Mr. Erickson then writes:

- The Trinity is incomprehensible. We cannot fully understand the mystery of the Trinity (page 104).

It is not a mystery; it was an incorrect assumption by early theologians, carried on today by tradition.

This next statement of Mr. Erickson (page 105) has multiple gods, three, in addition to a triune god.

- Each of the three, Father, Son, and Holy Spirit, is to be worshiped, as is the Triune God.

The more one tries to explain trinity, the more elaborate and weird the statements.

Mr. Erickson ends this chapter with a paraphrased quote:

- As some has said of this doctrine [trinity]: Try to explain it, and you'll lose your mind; but try to deny it, and you'll lose your soul.[109]

Not denying, but refuting, Isaiah says it best:

→ For to us a child is born, to us a son is given, and the government will be on his shoulders. And he will be called Wonderful Counselor, Mighty God, Everlasting Father, Prince of Peace.[110]

Jesus said:

→ And do not call anyone on earth "father," for you have one Father, and he is in heaven.[111]

---

109 *Introducing Christian Doctrine*, page 105
110 Bible, Isaiah 9:6
111 Bible, Matthew 23:9

Why would Isaiah call Jesus "Everlasting Father" when Jesus said there is only one Father? And why, in John 14:26, did Jesus say that the Father would send the Counselor, and then in John 16:7, He said that He, Jesus, would send Him? If there is a trinity, someone made a mistake in these two verses. They seemingly contradict one another. But there is no mistake to be found when we realize that our Father in heaven visited us as the man Jesus and now lives in us as the Holy Spirit.

3. Systematic Theology[112]

Chapter XVII. Introduction to Trinitarianism (page 272).

In his 17th chapter, under the subtitle "Introduction to Trinitarianism," Lewis Sperry Chafer quotes a statement of a Dr. W. Lindsay Alexander:

- Whilst, then, we admit that the doctrine of the Trinity does not stand on exactly the same ground as the doctrines formally enunciated in Scripture, we claim for it an equal authority on the ground that it lies involved in the statements of Scripture, and is the proper evolution and expression of these. As a doctrine it is a human induction from the statements of Scripture; but the induction being fairly made, it is as much a part of God's teaching in His word as is any of those doctrines which He has formally enunciated there.[113]

Chafer then goes on to state:

- The doctrine of the Trinity is drawn wholly from revelation.[114]

Mr. Chafer contradicts himself by first stating that human beings came to a conclusion from what is read in the Scriptures, and then secondly, stating that the doctrine of the trinity is a revelation from God.

---

112 Lewis Sperry Chafer, *Systematic Theology*, Publisher Kregel Publications, 1993, ISBN - 0825423406

113 *Systematic Theology*, page 272

114 *Systematic Theology*, page 273

41

The idea or concept of trinity has never been a revelation from God. It has always been a conclusion that man has come to from his attempt to understand God from man's perspective. In other words, not man made in the image of God, but God made in the image of man.

Here is an example from Chafer's book:

- Various illustrations of such realities in nature might be introduced. In the constitution of a human being there is conjunction of unity and plurality. The immaterial and material elements combine to form one individual. Each of these elements is essential to human existence in this sphere. Thus it is seen that a human being may be singular in one sense and plural in another. If plurality and unity are both required in human existence, why should plurality and unity be denied in the case of the divine existence? Should it be supposed that God may include in His creature what He cannot manifest in Himself? By this analogy no attempt is made to demonstrate that a human person combining in himself the material and immaterial is comparable as to elements or order with three persons subsisting in one divine Essence. The analogy goes no further than to establish a principle. In the case of the human being, there is one consciousness with a twofold subsistence; in the case of Deity, there are three consciousnesses and but one nature. The principle that plurality is not incompatible with unity is thus proved.[115] (page 275)

Here we can see that Mr. Chafer – as well as so many others before him – has tried to explain what God is by what he sees man is. God is Spirit, and when He inhabited flesh, He then appeared to be in this particular form of "plurality" that Chafer infers to. God is not a plurality, but was inhabiting a body. Even we humans are only inhabiting a fleshly "tent" – both Paul and Peter referred to our bodies as tents – (2 Corinthians 5:1 and 2 Peter 1:3). God is Spirit; He:

→ ...became flesh and lived for a while among us.[116]

---

115 *Systematic Theology*, page 275
116 Bible, John 1:14

Mr. Chafer wrote:

- ...three persons subsisting in one divine Essence.[117]

If the dictionary definition of the word *essence* is: *an existent being; especially, an immaterial being – spirit*, then is he trying to say that we have three beings living in one being? Three spirits living in one spirit? This belief of Mr. Chafer brings him to make this statement:

- Those who oppose the doctrine of the Trinity automatically reject the Deity of the Son and the Spirit.[118]

There is no rejection of the Deity of Christ without the trinity; on the contrary, Jesus is actually realized for who He really is – God. Trinitarians actually put Jesus in a secondary position, subject to the Father, but in reality He is the Father. God, our Father Creator, became flesh as the man Jesus and now lives in us as the Holy Spirit. His name is Jesus, Yah-saves.

→ The Lord is the Spirit.[119]

4. *A Systematic Theology of the Christian Religion*[120]

In his third chapter titled "Doctrine of the Trinity," James Oliver Buswell Jr. wrote:

- ...these three are one God the same in substance, equal in power and glory.[121]

This substance of which God is made of is Spirit. If theologians would use the word spirit instead of substance, essence, subsistence, nature, and other such terms, there wouldn't be so much confusion in theology.

---

117 *Systematic Theology,* page 275

118 *Systematic Theology,* page 279

119 Bible, 2 Corinthians 3:17

120 James Oliver Buswell Jr., *A Systematic Theology of the Christian Religion,* Publisher Zondervan, 1962, ISBN- 13 - 9780370221906

121 *A Systematic Theology of the Christian Religion,* page 102

When using the correct terminology, what Buswell in writing "same in substance" has stated here is: "same in spirit" – three Spirits, tritheism.

If these "three" are equal in power, then the Son would have had authority to send the Father, a ridiculous concept to us. When appearing as a man, Jesus said:

→   …the Father is greater than I.[122]

On page 102 Buswell writes:

•   The Being of God is complex.

The word *complex* according to the dictionary: *consisting of various connected or interwoven parts; composite. Composite* from the dictionary: *made up of separate parts or elements; combined or compounded.* God is one, not parts.

"Jesus is Jahweh." [Yahweh] Under this heading, Buswell, quoting from various passages of Scripture, has rightly stated that Jesus is Yahweh. He comes to this conclusion:

•   These passages indicate that Christ and God and Jahweh are one.[123]

Buswell has not included the words *Holy Spirit* or *Father.* Had he done so, we would see that, according to his reasoning, there must be five persons who are one. If, in his belief that God is three persons, and that Jesus is Yahweh, what name would he then call the Father of Jesus?

Thinking of God as three persons creates multiple problems in explaining Him. Believing in God's word that God is one is far simpler. God our Father, who is Spirit, was in the flesh as the man Jesus, and now lives in us. He is the Holy Spirit, not an evil spirit or some other spirit, but the Holy Spirit. God is Spirit.

---

122   Bible, John 14:28

123   *A Systematic Theology of the Christian Religion,* page 105

In explaining the Holy Spirit, Buswell states:

- I have translated the last preposition in this passage (John 14:15–17) "among" rather than "in." Grammatically of course the prepositional phrase might be construed distributively, "in you individually," but the context indicates no such thought. He is to be "with you forever." You already "know him" because "he dwells with you," and he is going to be among you or "in you as a company." [124](page 115)

Changing the words changes the meaning. Here we can see that with a preconceived idea of trinity, Buswell could not understand this verse and had to change the verse to fit his belief. The word *in* from this verse means exactly that, in, not among. God dwells in us.

If Buswell had also looked at the following verses, he would see that Jesus was talking of Himself as Spirit, not as human:

→ I will not leave you as orphans; I will come to you. Before long, the world will not see me anymore, but you will see me.[125]

That is, seeing the Spirit, not the flesh.

On page 121, Buswell states:

- Jahweh promises to send the Messiah and the Messiah's name will be "Jahweh our righteousness." This means that the Messiah whom Jahweh God will send will himself be Jahweh God.

How does this man make this true statement that Yahweh, our Father in heaven, is the one in the fleshly body called Jesus (Yahweh-saves), and yet calls God more than one – a trinity? God the Father is God the Son and is the Holy Spirit in us, because God is Spirit.

In this next statement Buswell comes close to the beliefs of the Jehovah's Witnesses.

---

124 *A Systematic Theology of the Christian Religion*, page 115
125 Bible, John 14:18,19

- Since Jahweh is translated Kyrios in the Septuagint, it is my conviction that when Paul says, "the Lord [Kyrios] is the Spirit," (2Cor. 3:17) he means us to understand, Jahweh is the name of the Holy Spirit, just as truly as the name of the Father and of the Son. The "name," not "names" of the Father and of the Son and of the Holy Spirit in which we are to be baptized, is to be understood as Jahweh, the name of the Triune God.[126]

Here we can see that Buswell has the right idea of a singular name when speaking of the name in Matthew 28:19. But he chose the wrong name. Yahweh means *I am*, Jesus means "I am-saves." (Yah-saves) If we call upon God using the name Yahweh, we are ignoring His death on the cross for us. If we call upon God using the name Jesus (Yah-saves), we are acknowledging His payment for our sins by His death on the cross for us.

The word *Kyrios* in Greek means *Lord*; only the Old Testament translated the word *Yahweh* as *Lord*, not the New Testament.

5. *Practical Christian Theology*[127]

- The Triunity of God's Person.

Under this subtitle, Floyd H. Barackman writes these words:

- Triunity speaks of there being three Persons, simultaneously possessing the one divine essence.

Again, the dictionary definition of the words are needed here:

Essence – *an existent being, especially, an immaterial being--spirit.*

Person – *any human being* [God is the Supreme Being] *considered as a distinct entity or personality; an individual.*

---

126 *A Systematic Theology of the Christian Religion*, page 123

127 Floyd H. Barackman, *Practical Christian Theology*, Published by Fleming H. Revell, 1984, ISBN - 10: 0800713729

Trinity – *the state or character of being three; any union of three parts or elements in one.*

Unity – *the state or fact of being one or, the condition or fact of being free from variety or diversity.*

In the preceding quotation from Barackman, he has three beings possessing another being. The Bible says that God is Spirit; He does not possess a spirit. The word *trinity* is a union of parts into a whole; God is indivisible, no parts. He is not composed of parts. Jesus prefaced His most important commandment with the statement:

→ The Lord our God is one.

Mr. Barackman wrote the subtitle:

• 3b. The Relation of the Persons within the Godhead

Under this title he wrote:

• The Scriptures show a subordination among the members of the Godhead.

But then he also wrote that these "members" have:

• Equal qualities and powers.

These statements prove a real contradiction in concepts. The dictionary definition of the word *subordinate* is: *Belonging to an inferior or lower order in a classification; secondary. Subject or subservient to another.* If one "member" of the "Godhead" is subservient to the other, "he" or "they" most certainly are not equal in power since one has command over the other. Jesus, *when in the form of a man*, said:

→ My Father is greater than I.[128]

---

128 Bible, John 14:28

Only if the Son could send the Father could there be equality in a trinity.

6. *Foundations of the Christian Faith*[129]

In the beginning of chapter 10 of his book, James Montgomery Boice explains "trinity" as coming from the Latin word trinitas, which he said means "threeness," but Jesus gave the first and most important commandment (quoting Moses):

→ Hear O Israel, the Lord our God is one.

On page 115, section 4, Boice writes:

• ...the Father (not the Spirit) sent the Son.

If God is Spirit then the Father is Spirit. The word *Holy* is not part of a name; it is an adjective describing the word *Spirit*. God is a Holy Spirit. God, our Father in heaven, is the Holy Spirit. 2 Corinthians 3:17 tells us that:

→ The Lord is the Spirit.

So, Jesus being the Lord, is the Spirit – the Holy Spirit. If not, then we would have three spirits to deal with – tritheism – three gods.

Summary of Chapter 2

The writers or teachers of the six books quoted here have done their best to explain what man has taught them to believe, using a variety of words that do not work. It would have been far better if these writers would have believed no man but had asked Jesus to teach them the truth. Jesus' apostle, John, when writing to the Church stated the following:

---

129 James Montgomery Boice, *Foundations of the Christian Faith*, Publisher Intervarsity Press, ISBN - 10 0877849919

→ I am writing these things to you about those who are trying to lead you astray. As for you, the anointing you received from Him [Jesus] remains in you, and you do not need anyone to teach you.[130]

And Jesus' apostle, James, wrote:

→ If any of you lacks wisdom, let him ask of God.[131]

Jesus said:

→ If anyone loves me, he will obey my teaching. My Father will love him, and we will come to him and make our home with him.[132]

Jesus is talking about Himself both as man and God, our Father in heaven, coming to live in us as Spirit – the Holy Spirit. He stated:

→ Whoever has my commands and obeys them, he is the one who loves me. He who loves me, will be loved by my Father, and I too will love him and show myself to him.[133]

He shows Himself when He comes to live in us as the Holy Spirit.

→ In Christ all the fullness of the Deity lives in bodily form.[134]

That is, God in the flesh.

God is not a trinity of three persons or beings as the "Godhead," (a King James Version term) but is a singular person/being who is Spirit and has revealed Himself in a human body. The only reason the trinity is difficult to understand is because it does not exist. There are not "three that bear record in heaven" as written in the King James Version of the Bible. (More on this later in this summary.) Jesus is called:

---

130 Bible, John 2:26,27
131 Bible, James 1:5
132 Bible, John 14:23
133 Bible, John 14:21
134 Bible, Colossians 2:9

→ Father – Everlasting Father (Isaiah 9:6).

→ The Word – The Word became flesh (John 1:1).

→ The Spirit – The Lord [Jesus] is the Spirit (2 Corinthians 3:17).

God Himself came to His children to teach us how to relate to Him. Just as a man relates to his parents as their son; to his children as their father, and to his wife as her husband, so too does God relate to us. He relates to us as our Creator (the Father); He relates to us as our fellow man or brother (the Son), and He relates to us as our Counselor (the Holy Spirit).

We have read/heard about God as our Creator/Father in heaven, we saw Him as a perfect man (an example for us), and now we can know Him as the indwelling Spirit in us *if* we are "born again."

→ One God and Father of all, who is over all and through all and in all.[135]

That is, in all born-again Christians, not all people.

This mistaken doctrine of a trinity, a god that is three persons in one, made over 1600 years ago, is a stumbling block for Jews, Muslims, Catholics, Mormons, Jehovah's Witnesses, and many denominations in Christian churches; consequently, all believe that, *they only*, have the truth.

Back in the early 1500s, Martin Luther checked out the religious leaders of his day. By reading the Bible, he managed to find out that those who were in charge of the Church, whether they understood it or not, were misleading the public, and this for hundreds of years. It was the start of the Reformation. Today, there is still need of reform.

The New Testament was written, not by God, but by men inspired by God. The writers were men doing their best to bring the truth to us.

---

135 Bible, Ephesians 4:6

Man is not perfect and can make mistakes. Our various Bibles are not perfect, but the truth most certainly can be found within them.

Here are three mistakes to show that the Bible is not perfect: the first one is not worrisome; the second one *is* significant; however, the third mistake, found in the King James Version, is of much more consequence.

1. Some long-ago writer made a simple error when quoting the Old Testament. It is not that important, but every Bible translator copied this same mistake. Here is the original verse that was quoted:

→ I will put my law in their minds and write it on their hearts.[136]

And now here is the first New Testament quotation of this verse:

→ I will put my laws in their minds and write them on their hearts.[137]

But, two chapters later, this quotation has become the following:

→ I will put my laws in their hearts and write them on their minds.[138]

This mistake was a simple reversal of the words *minds* and *hearts*, it's not that important.

2. Mark, not having the advantage of the New Testament as we do, may not have understood who the man Jesus really was, so he writes:

→ It is written in Isaiah the Prophet: "I will send my messenger [John the Baptist] before you, who will prepare your way."[139]

Mark (or the translators) makes the mistake of saying this verse was found in Isaiah, but more importantly, he misquotes the verse:

---

136 Bible, Jeremiah 31:33
137 Bible, Hebrews 8:10
138 Bible, Hebrews 10:16
139 Bible, Mark 1:2

→ "I will send my messenger, who will prepare the way before me," says the LORD Almighty.[140]

Mark misquotes the word *me* and instead writes *you*, and, *your*.

3. Those in authority in the Roman Catholic Church would have us believe that their traditional teaching is more important than the Bible, so that whatever they proclaim, takes precedence over what is written. But, anyone reading the Bible can see that the first churches were formed during and from the teachings of Jesus and His apostles (His disciples, some apostles, wrote the New Testament), prior to the Roman Catholic Church being formed (it being a takeover of the church by the Roman Empire in the fourth century A.D.).

The Bible was written in Hebrew (Old Testament) and Greek (New Testament) and was not translated into Latin until about 400 years after Jesus and His apostles lived. When Jerome translated the Greek Scriptures into the Latin Vulgate for the Roman Catholic Church (about 400 A.D.), the verse now found in the King James Version of the Bible, 1 John 5:7, did not exist. This extracanonical verse was written thusly:

- There are three that bear record in heaven: the Father, the Word, and the Holy Ghost, and these three are one.[141]

Later Vulgate manuscripts not only had this verse added to them (about 1523 A.D.), but had the word *me* left out of John 14:14:

→ You may ask *me* for anything in my name, and I will do it.

There are some Christians who believe that the King James Version is the only correct version. The King James "Authorized" Version, was authorized by King James, not by God. The translators of the King James Version of the Bible wrote:

---

140   Bible, Malachi 3:1
141   King James Bible, 1 John 5:7

- We hold it our duty to offer it to Your Majesty [King James], not only to our King and Sovereign, but as to the principal Mover and Author of the work (found in the Epistle Dedicatory of the King James Bible: see Appendix).

If today's Evangelical Christians were to declare truthfully that God is one, and that the only name to call upon Him for salvation was Jesus (Yahweh-saves), then "Christian" religious cults could find the truth (Catholics, Mormons, Jehovah's Witnesses, etc. More on this later). And, maybe the Jews would accept their Messiah – Jesus, if Christians would present Jesus/Yahweh as one and the same God. Jesus said:

→ I and the Father are one.[142]

How can the Jews or Muslims, who rightly believe that God is one, ever believe in the "Christian" doctrine of a triune God? When Jesus was asked:

→ Of all the commandments, which is the most important?[143]

His answer was:

→ The most important one is this: "Hear, O Israel, the Lord our God, the Lord is one. Love the Lord your God with all your heart and with all your soul and with all your mind and with all your strength." The second is this: "Love your neighbor as your-self." There is no commandment greater than these.[144]

The Qur'an, or, Koran (same book, different translation of its Arabic title, what Muslims believe to be the "word of God") has more than fifty verses *disclaiming* God having partners. From the Qur'an:

- Unbelievers too are those who said that Allah is a third of three [trinity].[145]

---

142 Bible, John 10:30
143 Bible, Mark 12:28
144 Bible, Mark 12:29,30,31
145 Qur'an, 5:73

- Keep in mind, when Allah will ask Jesus son of Mary; Didst thou say to the people: Take me and my mother for two gods beside Allah?[146]

- They do blaspheme who say: Allah is one of three in a Trinity. For there is no God except one God.[147]

Christians who claim God to be a trinity, three persons in one, are stumbling blocks to Muslims who rightly believe that God is one.

Because a Muslim's religious belief permeates all their life (social, political, governmental, educational, and so on), they see the Western world as living the same way. For the sake of Muslims (and many others), Christians need to stand out as separate from the Western governments, which legally allow gambling, pornography, excessive alcohol consumption, same-sex marriage, abortion, euthanasia, and so on.

The Bible tells us to obey the governing authorities, it doesn't tell us to be unequally yoked with them. Our governments are too corrupt; we need, as the Bible states, to "come out from among them." Jesus said we are to be "in the world" but not "of the world." Being patriotic or devoted to one's country can get in the way of being devoted to Christ.

This doctrine of the trinity created by the Roman Catholic Church, being a stumbling block to Muhammad and his followers, was instrumental in the creation of Islam's Qur'an. The next chapter, *The Qur'an*, will explore verses from the Qur'an that will verify this last statement.

---

146 Muhammad Zafrulla Khan, *The Qur'an*, Published by Olive Branch Press, 1970, ISBN - 9781566562554 chapter 5:116

147 Yusuf Ali *The Holy Qur'an, text, translation & commentary*, published by Kamil Muslim Trust, 1935, ISBN - 0915957760, chapter 5:76

CHAPTER 3 - THE QUR'AN

The main quotations from the Qur'an will be from Majid Fakhry's translation of the Qur'an.[148] The following words are written on the back of the book cover: "approved by Al-Azhar University, the chief center of Islamic and Arabic learning in the world." To clarify the understanding of what is being stated in the Qur'an, there will be various quotations from Muhammad Zafrulla Kahn's translation[149] designated here as – *MZK*. There will also be a few quotations from Abdullah Yusuf Ali's translation[150] designated – *Koran*.

---

148 Majid Fakhry, *An Interpretation of the Qur'an*, New York University Press, copyright 2000, 2004,

149 Muhammad Zafrulla Khan, *The Qur'an*, published 1970 by Olive Branch Press, ISBN - 9781566562554

150 Kamil Muslim Trust, *The Holy Qur'an, text, translation, & commentary*, 1935, ISBN - 915957760

The Qur'an states that the author Muhammad was illiterate (chapter 29 vs.48, and chapter 7 vs.157, 158). Muhammad taught his disciples his "revelations from God," but it was his disciples who wrote down the Qur'an.

This chapter will be similar to chapter 1 of Part 2 in that it will have subtitles. For each of these subtitles, not only will there be comparative verses from the Qur'an, but there will be a comparison of Qur'anic verses to Biblical verses.

Christians will note that the word Gospel is used in this chapter slightly differently from what they are used to. The reason for this is that Muslim readers who are used to the Qur'an, may understand it differently.

The Qur'an does not use the word *chapter* in it. It uses the word *sura* where we would write the word *chapter*. This book will use the word *chapter* for clarity.

1. God is one

Both the Islamic Qur'an (from the prophet Muhammad) and the Christian Bible state that God is one. About 600 years before the Qur'an was written down, the Gospel of Jesus affirmed Moses' teaching that God is one. When Jesus was asked:

→ Of all the commandments, which is the most important?[151]

His answer was:

→ The most important one is this: "Hear O Israel, the Lord our God, the Lord is one. Love the Lord your God with all your heart and with all your soul and with all your mind and with all your strength." The second is this: "Love your neighbor as yourself." There is no greater commandment than these.[152]

---

151 Bible, Mark 12:28
152 Bible, Mark 12:29,30,31

These two commandments originally came from God – through Moses – about 2050 years before the Qur'an was written.

The statement: "God has no partners," found many times throughout the Qur'an, overemphasizes the oneness of God, and for good reason; Muhammad was not arguing against Christian teaching – the Gospel of Jesus, but against a false doctrine in Christianity – the trinity and the supposed importance of Mary. In the Qur'an, it is written:

- O Jesus, son of Mary, did you say to the people: "Take me and my mother as gods, apart from Allah?"[153]

It is quite understandable after centuries of the Roman Catholic Church's false teaching of a triune God, carried on by today's evangelical Christians (with Mary being revered by Catholics, much, if not more, than God), that the author of the Qur'an would be adamant in the oneness of God. In later years a verse was mistakenly added to the King James Version of the Gospel:

- For there are three that bear record in heaven: the Father, the Word, and the Holy Ghost, and these three are one.[154]

Nowhere in the Gospels (Bible) does it say that God is more than one. (For more on the false doctrine of trinity, see chapter 2 of Part 2.)

2. Abraham, Father of many Nations

Muhammad claimed Abraham was a Muslim:

- Abraham was neither a Jew nor a Christian, but a hanif (one who turns from paganism) and a Muslim (one who believes in the unity of Allah).[155]

---

153   Qur'an 5:16
154   King James Bible, 1 John 5,7
155   Qur'an, 3:67

- Abraham was neither a Jew nor a Christian; he was ever inclined to Allah and obedient to Him, and he was not of those who associate partners with Allah.[156][MZK]

- Abraham was not a Jew nor yet a Christian; but he was true in Faith, and bowed his will to Allah's, and he joined not gods with Allah.[157] [Koran]

Here we can see that neither the translators, nor Muhammad, read the Biblical Scriptures in searching for the truth. Neither Jew nor Christian would believe that Abraham was called a Jew or a Christian; Abraham lived long before the words *Jew* and *Christian* were ever spoken. The word *Jew* comes from *Judaite* (descendant of Judah). The Jews of today are the descendants of – and named after – Judah, a *descendant* of Abraham.

The Bible tells us that Abraham fathered the Jews through his son Isaac's descendants, and fathered the Arabs (Muslims) through his son Ishmael's (Isma'il's) descendants.

Christians are named after the Christ (Messiah) – Jesus, the one prophesied in Jewish Scripture by Moses, David, Isaiah, Zechariah, and Malachi. Jesus came 1450 years after Abraham lived.

3. Scriptural Authority

Each of these three religious group's books state the unity or oneness of God, and if the word *Muslim* meant "one who believes in the unity of God," as Muhammad has stated, then Jews and non-trinitarian Christians must be "Muslims" too. But if the word *Muslim* means those who follow the teaching of Muhammad, then Abraham was most certainly not a Muslim either since Muhammad lived many years after Abraham.

---

156 Muhammad Zafrulla Khan, *The Qur'an*, Published by Olive Branch Press, 1970, ISBN - 9781566562554 chapter 3:67

157 Abdulla Yusuf Ali, *The Holy Koran, text, translation & commentary*, Published by Kamil Muslim Trust, 1935, ISBN - 0915957760 chapter 3:67

Assuming both Abraham and his sons would have spoken the same language, it is probable that the Arabic word for God, Allah, comes from an earlier Hebrew (Chaldean or Babylonian) word for God, אכה (ĕlᴈhh), pronounced el-aw', which sounds like Allah.

Even though Muhammad states that "Allah is one God,"[158] Allah is often referred to in both singular and plural in the Qur'an: *I, My, He, Him, His, We, Our.*

The "We" in the following verses is supposed to be Allah/God speaking.

- We have provided from Our Bounty a fair provision.[159]

- We have indeed brought Moses the Book.[160]

- We gave the Children of Israel the Book, the Judgement and the Prophecy.[161]

- We have indeed given Moses the Book. We also gave Jesus, son of Mary, clear signs (miracles) and strengthened him with the Holy Spirit.[162]

- We gave David a Book. We gave David the Psalms.[163]

- We sent Jesus, son of Mary, confirming what he had before him of the Torah, and We gave him the Gospel, wherein is guidance and light.[164]

However, why would a Muslim read the Gospel "wherein is guidance and light" when they have been instructed by Muhammad that the

---

158 Koran, 2:224 & 4:171

159 Qur'an, 16:75

160 Qur'an, 25:35

161 Qur'an, 45:16

162 Qur'an, 2:87

163 Qur'an, 4:163 & 17:55

164 Qur'an, 5:46

books of the Jews and Christians have been corrupted? The Qur'an also states:

- We gave him [Jesus] the Gospel.[165]

In the preceding verses, the author of the Qur'an claims that God had previously given us books, the Torah, the Psalms, and the Gospel (collectively, found in the Bible), so that we could know the truth about God. But Muhammad also says:

- And this (the Qur'an) is a revelation of the Lord of the Worlds. And it is, indeed, in the Scriptures of the ancients.[166]

- Surely, it is mentioned in the former Scriptures. Is it not a sign for them that the scholars of the Children of Israel recognize it?[167] [MZK]

But nowhere, in any of the former Scriptures (the Bible or Torah), is the Qur'an ever mentioned, and as for recognizing it, neither Jew nor Christian would recognize the Qur'an as being from God.

4. God's Word Never Changes

Here are three statements about God's immutability:

- You are not told except what was told to the Messengers before you.[168]

- Nothing is said to thee but that which was said to the Messengers before thee.[169] [MZK]

(Why the old English style "thee" in a 1970 translation of Arabic?)

---

165 Qur'an, 57:27
166 Qur'an, 26:192,196,197
167 MZK, 26:192,196,197
168 Qur'an, 41:43
169 MZK, 41:43

- Those to whom We have given the Book (the Torah) know that it is revealed from your Lord in truth. The Word of your Lord has been completed in truth and justice; no one can change His Words.[170]

- It is Allah's Way which has gone before; and you will never find any alteration of Allah's Way.[171]

Here is Allah telling Muhammad, that he, Muhammad, has not been told anything new that hasn't been taught before, and that Allah's/God's word doesn't change. (Why the Qur'an then? There would be no need for a Qur'an.) But, he then contradicts himself by stating that Allah/God does change the verses or commandments:

- And if We replace a verse by another…Say: "The Holy Spirit (the angel Gabriel) has brought it down from your Lord in truth."[172]

- When We substitute in the Qur'an one commandment in place of another in older Scriptures, tell them the Spirit of Holiness has brought it down from thy Lord in accordance with the requirements of truth and wisdom.[173] [MZK]

Most of the verses in the Qur'an that make reference to Biblical verses, change the original meanings of the verses. Many of the commands that Muhammad gave contradict the Torah and the Gospel found in the Bible. Both Moses (in the Torah) and Jesus (in the Gospel) tell us that God's most important commandments are to love God and love your neighbor, but Muhammad tells his people to fight those who don't follow his commands.

Jesus said:

→ Do not think that I have come to abolish the Law or the Prophets; I have not come to abolish them but to fulfill them.

---

170 Qur'an, 6:114,115
171 Qur'an, 48:23
172 Qur'an, 16:101,102
173 MZK, 16:101,102

I tell you the truth, until heaven and earth disappear, not the smallest letter, not the least stroke of a pen, will by any means disappear from the Law until everything is accomplished.[174]

God's commandments never change. When Jesus brought the Gospel message He did not change or add a single one of God's commandments; rather, He fulfilled them. The commandments Jesus gave were not new; they came from the Torah.

5. Prophets

When speaking of prophets Muhammad includes Ishmael as a prophet of God:

- And remember Isma'il, Elias and Dhul-Kifl; each was one of the pious.[175]

- Call to mind also Ishmael and Isaiah and Ezekiel.[176] [MZK]

- Ishmael and Elisha and Ezekiel.[177] [Koran]

The three translators of the Qur'an/Koran do not agree on this second name.

Isaiah, Ezekiel, Elisha, and Elias (Elias is Greek for the Hebrew Elijah) were all recorded as prophets in the older Scriptures (Old Testament portion of the Bible), and even though the Bible records thirty-nine prophets who served God, Ishmael (Isma'il) wasn't one of them.

According to the Torah (Genesis, Exodus, Leviticus, Numbers, and Deuteronomy) and the Bible, God made Ishmael a father of a great nation of desert dwellers (Arabs), but He did not make Ishmael a prophet.

---

174 Bible, Matthew 5:17,18
175 Qur'an, 38:48
176 MZK, 38:48
177 Koran, 38:48

> → And as for Ishmael, I will surely bless him; I will make him fruitful and will greatly increase his numbers. He will be the father of twelve rulers, and I will make him into a great nation. But my covenant I will establish with Isaac...an everlasting covenant.[178]

The Scriptures (the Bible) state that Elias (Elijah), Ezekiel, and Isaiah, were prophets from God. There is no mention in the Qur'an, other than this one time in MZK's translation, of Isaiah's name. It is a surprise to see Isaiah's name at all in the Qur'an, because Isaiah is the one who foretold the coming of Jesus as "son," "Counselor," "God," and "Father."

In both the Jewish Scripture and the Christian Bible, Moses, David, Isaiah, Zechariah, and Malachi, all prophesied of the Messiah to come – Jesus. But it was Isaiah who made the most explicit prophecy. Thirteen hundred years before the Qur'an was written, and 700 years before Jesus came, Isaiah prophesied that Jesus would come:

> → For to us a child is born, to us a son is given, and the government will be on his shoulders. And he will be called Wonderful Counselor, Mighty God, Everlasting Father, Prince of Peace.[179]

He also wrote:

> → The Lord Himself will give you a sign: The virgin will be with child and will give birth to a son, and will call him Immanuel.[180] [*Immanuel* means *God with us*.]

From the Qur'an, Muhammad states:

> • And We made Mary's son [Jesus] and his mother a Sign.[181]

Although the Bible does not call Ismael a prophet, Muhammad includes Ishmael's name in his list of the prophets. In the Qur'an, Muhammad calls Ishmael:

---

178   Bible, Genesis 18:20,21
179   Bible, Isaiah 9:6
180   Bible, Isaiah 7:14
181   Qur'an, 23:50

- A messenger and a prophet.[182]

- An apostle and a prophet.[183] [MZK]

For what other reason would he make these two statements other than self-justification?

6. The *Seal*, or, Last of the Prophets

Muhammad claimed to be a prophet.

- And to those who follow the Messenger, the unlettered [illiterate] Prophet [Muhammad] whom they find mentioned in their Torah and Gospel.[184]

- Say: "O people, I am Allah's Messenger to you all. Believe in Allah and His Messenger, the unlettered Prophet...follow him, that perchance you may be well-guided."[185] [Allah speaking to Muhammad.]

- Jesus, son of Mary, said: "O Children of Israel, I am Allah's Messenger to you, confirming what came before me of the Torah, and announcing the news of a Messenger who will come after me, whose name is Ahmad."[186]

- ...fulfilling the prophecies contained in the Torah...[187] [MZK]

- Muhammad is not the father of any of your men, but is the Messenger of Allah and the seal [last] of the prophets.[188]

---

182   Qur'an, 19:54
183   Koran, 19:54
184   Qur'an, 7:57
185   Qur'an, 7:158
186   Qur'an, 61:6
187   MZK, 61:6
188   Qur'an, 33:40

These verses have Allah telling the prophet Muhammad to proclaim that all believers should follow Muhammad, and that he, Muhammad, was mentioned in the Bible. But nowhere in the Gospels or the Torah (collectively called the Bible) is found the name "Ahmad," or any other verse referring to future prophets. The only one mentioned in the Torah and the Gospel is the Messiah – Jesus.

Jesus fulfilled the prophecies, in the Torah, of a future prophet. Fulfilled means completed. Jesus did not tell of a future prophet, but rather that He Himself is coming back. Jesus is the last true prophet. The only prophet mentioned in the Bible after Jesus, is the one in the book of Revelation – the false prophet.

In the following verses, the author of the Qur'an, Muhammad, is promoting the idea that his coming was predicted by Jesus in the Scriptures.

- Have you considered? What if it be from Allah and you disbelieve in it, while a witness from the Children of Israel bears witness to the like of it and believes, whereas you wax proud.[189]

- If my [Muhammad] revelation is from Allah, and you reject it, would it not be strange that a witness from among the children of Israel should have foretold the advent of one like himself and should have believed in him, while you deny him [Muhammad] in your arrogance?[190][MZK]

Jesus did not foretell of a future prophet, but only that He, Jesus, would return.

7. Muhammad's Qur'an vs. Jesus' Gospel

Here Muhammad claims the superiority of the Qur'an:

---

189 Qur'an, 46:10
190 MZK, 46:10

- It is He [Allah] Who sent forth His Messenger [Muhammad] with the guidance and the religion of truth, that He may exalt it above every other religion.[191]

- ...that He may cause it to prevail over all other religions.[192] [MZK]

- And before it [the Qur'an], there came the Book of Moses, as a guidance and a mercy; and this is a corroborating Book in Arabic tongue.[193]

- Before it [the Qur'an] was the Book of Moses, a guide and a mercy; and this is a Book in Arabic fulfilling previous Books.[194] [MZK]

- We have revealed to you [Muhammad] the Book in truth, confirming the Scriptures that preceded it and superceding [sic] it.[195]

Muhammad, the true author of the Qur'an, not Allah/God, although admitting the authority of the Scriptures, but wanting control over all religions, proclaims that the Qur'an changes and supersedes all previous Scriptures. He does not follow his own advice:

- There is one who disputes concerning Allah without any knowledge, or guidance, or an illuminating Book.[196]

- There are some among men who dispute concerning Allah without knowledge, without guidance, and without the authority of an enlightening Book, disdainfully, that they may lead people astray from Allah's way.[197] [MZK]

---

191 Qur'an, 48:28
192 MZK, 48:28
193 Qur'an, 46:12
194 MZK, 46:12
195 Qur'an, 5:48
196 Qur'an, 22:8
197 MZK, 22:8

In John's Gospel, Jesus states:

→ I am the way and the truth and the life. No one comes to the Father except through me. If you really knew me, you would know my Father as well.[198]

The Gospel of Jesus confirms, fulfills, and completes the Torah; the Qur'an contradicts the Torah and the Gospels.

8. Angel of Light

Muhammad proclaims his vision of the Holy Spirit:

• And if We replace a verse by another...Say: "The Holy Spirit (the angel Gabriel) has brought it down from your Lord in truth."[199]

• Tell them the Spirit of Holiness has brought it down from thy Lord.[200] [MZK]

• Holy Spirit.[201] [Koran]

• Do you, then, dispute with him (Muhammad) concerning what he saw. He has indeed seen him (Gabriel) a second time. He saw some of the Great Signs of his Lord.[202]

The Gospel states that Jesus is the Holy Spirit (2 Corinthians 3:17). Gabriel is an angel or archangel (the meaning of the word Gabriel, originating from Hebrew, is *valiant man of God*).

In Matthew's Gospel, Jesus said:

→ Many false prophets will appear and deceive many people.[203]

---

198 Bible, John 14:6
199 Qur'an, 16:102,102
200 MZK, 16:101,102
201 Koran, 16:102
202 Qur'an, 53:12,13,18
203 Bible, Matthew 24:11

Jesus' apostle Paul states:

→ For such men are false apostles, deceitful workmen, masquerading as apostles of Christ. And no wonder, for Satan himself masquerades as an angel of light. It is not surprising, then, if his servants masquerade as servants of righteousness.[204]

Did Muhammad see someone or something (Satan?). Being illiterate, and with no access to the Scriptures, Muhammad had nothing to test the validity of the information he claimed, or was given.

9. The Preservation of God's Word

Muhammad's promotion of the Qur'an as the word of God:

- It is truly We Who have revealed the Reminder [Qur'an], and We are truly its guardians.[205]

- Surely We ourself [sic] have sent down this Exhortation, and We will, most surely, safeguard it.[206] [MZK]

- Do you not know that Allah knows what is in the heavens and on earth. All that is in a Book; and that is an easy matter for Allah.[207]

- Knowest thou not that Allah knows whatsoever is in the heavens and the earth? Surely it is all preserved in a Book, and that is easy for Allah.[208] [MZK]

A book, translated from Arabic to English, by a man living in the twentieth century, published in 1970, would not naturally have old English "knowest" and "thou" in it. Somebody is trying to copy the style of the King James Bible to impress others.

---

204 Bible, 2 Corinthians 11:13,14,15
205 Qur'an, 15:9
206 MZK, 15:9
207 Qur'an, 22:70
208 MZK, 22:70

In these next verses Muhammad states that God can easily preserve His word, but contradicts himself when he claims that the Christians and Jews corrupted the Scriptures.

- There is a group of them who twist their tongues while reading the Book [Bible], so that you may suppose it is a part of the Book; whereas it is not a part of the Book. They also say: "It is from Allah," whereas it is not from Allah.[209]

- Woe unto those who write the Book with their hands, then say it is from Allah in order to sell it for a small price.[210]

Can God preserve His word or not? Yes! God had already safeguarded and preserved His word in a book – the Bible. It is the same now as it was hundreds of years before the Qur'an was written.

Here, Muhammad claims that God created the Qur'an.

- This Qur'an could never have been produced except by Allah. It is a confirmation of that (which was revealed) before it and an exposition of the Book. There is no doubt about it. It is from the Lord of the Worlds.[211]

- Do they not, then, ponder over the Qur'an? Had it been from someone other than Allah, they would have found in it many inconsistencies.[212]

As can be seen, there are many inconsistencies in the Qur'an; the Qur'an does not confirm the Scriptures (the Bible) written before it, it contradicts the Scriptures. From the New Testament:

- → I warn everyone who hears the words of the prophecy of this book: If anyone adds anything to them, God will add to him the plagues described in this book. And if anyone takes words away

---

209 Qur'an, 3:78
210 Qur'an, 2:79
211 Qur'an, 10:37
212 Qur'an, 4:82

from this book of prophecy, God will take away from him his share in the tree of life and in the holy city, which are described in this book.[213]

10. True Authority

Muhammad, although illiterate, wants all to follow the commands of a book, but which book?

- There is one who disputes concerning Allah without any knowledge, or guidance, or an illuminating Book.[214]

- There are some among men who dispute concerning Allah without knowledge, without guidance, and without the authority of an enlightening Book, disdainfully, that they may lead people astray from Allah's way.[215] [MZK]

- Say: "O People of the Book, you have nothing (that counts) until you observe the Torah and the Gospel and what has been revealed to you from your Lord."[216]

- Say to the People of the Book: "You have nothing to stand on until you carry out the commandments of the Torah and the Gospel."[217] [MZK]

Does this not also apply to Muhammad and Muslims?

In the Book of the "People of the Book," the Bible, Jesus said, quoting the Old Testament:

→ Love the Lord your God with all your heart and with all your soul and with all your mind. This is the first and

---

213 Bible, Revelation 22:18,19

214 Qur'an, 22:8

215 MZK, 22:8

216 Qur'an, 5:68

217 MZK, 5:68

greatest commandment. And the second is like it: Love your neighbor as yourself. All the Law and the Prophets hang on these two commandments.[218]

He also said:

→ Love your enemies and pray for those who persecute you.[219]

But Muhammad taught his followers to fight those who disagree with his beliefs.

The editors of Muhammad Zafrulla Khan's translation of the Qur'an wrote:

• The Qur'an is extremely concise and is a masterpiece of condensation. It leaves a great deal to the intelligence of the reader, urges reflection, and appeals constantly to the understanding.[220] [MZK]

In other words, it is very brief and you have to figure out what it means, so, those who are not educated or scholarly will have very little understanding of what they are reading. Besides, how would any human being know if it was condensed?

The Bible on the other hand, can be easily understood by anyone, educated or illiterate, simply by asking Jesus for help. The Bible verses were not designed to be interpreted by human reasoning; the meanings of the verses are revealed by God, when we ask Him. From the Bible:

→ If any of you lacks wisdom, he should ask God, who gives generously to all without finding fault, and it will be given to him.[221]

---

218 Bible, Mathew 22:37,38,39,40
219 Bible, Matthew 5:44
220 MZK, Preface, page ix, third from last paragraph
221 Bible, James 1:5

→ There is one God and one mediator between God and men, the man Jesus Christ, who gave himself as a ransom for all men.[222] (1 Timothy 2:5)

Why do Muslims not have to carry out the commandments of the Torah or the Gospel as the Qur'an instructs Christians and Jews? Even though the Qur'an states that Jesus was a prophet, Muhammad (and Muslims who follow his teachings), in ignoring the Gospels, practice hypocrisy because they are guilty of insinuating that Jesus was a liar. Jesus said:

→ I am the way and the truth and the life. No one comes to the Father except through me. If you really knew me, you would know my Father as well.[223]

The Qur'an creates oppressed slaves who must submit to false laws. The Gospel of Jesus creates willing servants who desire to serve God, not because they must submit, but because they love the Lord Jesus, who loved us first.

It is recorded in the Gospels that Jesus, who was more than a prophet: fed thousands, healed the sick, cured lepers, raised the dead, walked on water, and more importantly, rose from the dead. The "prophet" Muhammad could not perform any miracles or signs that would have witnessed to his prophetic office. He wrote contradictory to the segments of the Bible he supported. He changed God's word so as to enforce new ideas of his own. Who was the greater?

Muhammad was an illiterate man deceived by Satan, believing it was God who taught him the Qur'an, and, that he was a prophet who was to come. He was a self-proclaimed prophet just like Joseph Smith of the Mormons (more on this later). In the Gospel Jesus said:

→ Many false prophets will appear and deceive many people.[224]

---

222 Bible, 1 Timothy 2:5
223 Bible, John 14:6
224 Bible, Matthew 24:11

There is no longer need of a man as a prophet or teacher. Jesus said:

→ You are not to be called "Rabbi," for you have only one Master and you are all brothers. And do not call anyone on earth "father," for you have one Father and He is in heaven. Nor are you to be called "teacher," for you have one Teacher, the Christ.[225]

And Jesus' apostle John said:

→ As for you, the anointing [Holy Spirit] you received from him remains in you, and you do not need anyone to teach you.[226]

11. God's Name

Muhammad instructs Muslims to remember God's name.

- He who cleans himself shall prosper; remembering his Lord's name and praying. That, indeed, is in the ancient scrolls, the scrolls of Abraham and Moses.[227]

- He who purifies himself and remembers the name of his Lord and offers prayer will surely prosper. The same is set forth in the earlier Scriptures, the Scripture of Abraham and Moses.[228] [MZK]

As stated earlier, the word "Allah" probably comes from an old Hebrew word for "God." It is not a name.

In the earlier Scriptures, in Exodus 3:14, Moses asks God what His name is. God replies "Yahweh." (The Hebrew consonants are written YHWH; English renders it *Yahweh*.) Yahweh means *eternally self-existing* or "I am who I am." (Exodus 3:15) Yah is a contraction for Yahweh found in David's book of Psalms. Yah-saves (Yahweh-saves), or Yeshuä,

---

225 Bible, Matthew 23:8,9,10
226 Bible, 1 John 2:27
227 Qur'an, 87:14,15,18,19
228 MZK, 87:14,15,18,19

is rendered in English *Jesus* – I am – saves. To say the name *Jesus* is to say *Yahweh-saves*. Jesus, throughout the Gospels is called Savior.

Jesus, as a man, said:

→ Holy Father, protect them by the power of your name – your name which you have given me.[229]

The Bible states:

→ An angel of the Lord appeared to him [Joseph] in a dream and said: "Joseph, son of David, do not be afraid to take Mary home as your wife, because what is conceived in her is from the Holy Spirit. [The Immaculate Conception] She will give birth to a son, and you are to give him the name Jesus, because he will save his people from their sins."[230]

To call on the name Yahweh ignores the death on the cross He suffered for us. To call on the name Jesus acknowledges His love and forgiveness for us, and, His payment for our sins, *all* of our sins. But the Qur'an states:

• He [Allah] will forgive you some of your sins.[231]

This contradicts Jesus' teaching. Jesus' apostle Paul wrote:

→ Everyone who calls on the name of the Lord will be saved.[232]

12. Jesus as Man, Did Not Become God; God Came as the Man Jesus

Muhammad misunderstands:

---

229   Bible, John 17:11
230   Bible, Matthew 1:20,21
231   Qur'an, 46:31
232   Bible, Romans 10:13

- They [Christians] say: "The Compassionate [Allah] has taken to Himself a son."[233]

The Bible does not say that God took a son, but rather that God revealed Himself on earth to man, in the form of a man, as the "Son of God."

→ The Son is the radiance of God's glory and the exact representation of his being.[234]

→ In Christ all the fullness of the Deity lives in bodily form.[235]

The man Jesus was more than a prophet. God revealed the nature of His character to mankind the only way a man could understand: through another man – Jesus. God our Father creator, who is Spirit, the Holy Spirit, came to live on the earth as the man Jesus, an example for us of a man without sin. Jesus paid for our sins by dying on the cross for us, then rose again. Jesus said:

→ I am the resurrection and the life. He who believes in me will live, even though he dies; and whoever lives and believes in me will never die.[236]

Jesus' apostle Paul wrote:

→ For what I received I pass on to you as of first importance: that Christ died for our sins according to the Scriptures [Isaiah 53:1–12], that he was buried, that he was raised on the third day according to the Scriptures [Psalm 16:10], and that he appeared to Peter, and then to the Twelve [apostles].[237]

Jesus is the "Word" of God, the "Divine Expression." The Gospel of Jesus states:

---

233 Qur'an, 21:26
234 Bible, Hebrews 1:3
235 Bible, 2:9
236 Bible, John 11:25,26
237 Bible, 15:3,4,5

→ In the beginning was the Word, and the Word was with God, and the Word was God. The Word became flesh and lived for a while among us.[238]

Jesus, who is the Holy Spirit, comes to live inside our hearts, giving us the freedom and power to love others, even our enemies.

13. Violence vs. Love

Muhammad, through the Qur'an, taught violence. He created followers who are slaves to his laws.

- Fight those from among the People of the Book [Christians and Jews] who do not believe in Allah and the Last Day, nor do not forbid what Allah and His Messenger have forbidden and do not profess the true religion, till they pay the poll-tax out of hand and submissively.[239]

- Those who believe fight for the cause of Allah, and those who disbelieve, fight on behalf of the Devil. Fight then the followers of the Devil.[240]

- O Prophet, urge the believers to fight.[241]

- O Prophet, fight the unbelievers and the hypocrites and be stern with them. Their abode is Hell.[242]

- Allah has bought from the believers their lives and their wealth in return for Paradise; they fight in the Way of Allah, kill and get killed.[243]

---

238 Bible, John 1:1,14
239 Qur'an, 9:29
240 Qur'an, 4:76
241 Qur'an, 8:65
242 Qur'an, 9:73
243 Qur'an, 9:111

- O you who believe, fight those of the unbelievers who are near to you and let them see how harsh you can be.[244]

- Indeed, the punishment of those who fight Allah and His Messenger and go around corrupting the land is to be killed, crucified.[245]

The Qur'an calls God "the Compassionate One" and "the Merciful One," yet Muhammad taught his followers to be "harsh and stern," and to "fight and kill." Jesus, throughout the Bible and by living in us as the Holy Spirit, teaches us to be patient, kind, and gentle, loving one another, and yes, even loving our enemies. The first commandments God gave to Moses were:

→ The Lord our God, the Lord is one. Love the Lord with all your heart and with all your soul and with all your strength. Love your neighbor as yourself.[246]

In the Gospel of Jesus, when Jesus was asked what was the most important commandment, He said:

→ The most important one, is this: "Hear O Israel, the Lord our God, the Lord is one. Love the Lord your God with all your heart and with all your soul and with all your mind and with all your strength." The second is this: "Love your neighbor as yourself." There is no commandment greater than these.[247]

Here we see that Jesus repeats the original commands when He tells us to love God and love our neighbors.

When God commands: *Love God and Love your neighbor*, there is no need of laws stating: do not steal, or commit adultery, or kill, and so on. If I love my neighbor, I want him to enjoy his goods, his wife, and his life. But the Law will always exist for lawbreakers. Jesus said:

---

244 Qur'an, 9:123

245 Qur'an, 5:33

246 Bible, Deuteronomy 6:4,5 & Leviticus 19:18

247 Bible, Mark 12:29,30,31

→ Do not think that I have come to abolish the Law or the Prophets; I have not come to abolish them but to fulfill them. I tell you the truth, until heaven and earth disappear, not the smallest letter, not the least stroke of the pen, will by any means disappear from the Law until everything is accomplished.[248]

He also said:

→ In everything, do to others what you would have them do to you, for this sums up the Law and the Prophets.[249]

God says, that if we have need, simply ask of God who loves to give to our needs. Jesus our Lord loves us and desires a relationship with us. It is we who won't pay Him any attention.

→ If any of you lacks wisdom, he should ask God, who gives generously to all without finding fault, and it will be given to him.[250]

→ Whoever has my commands and obeys them, he is the one who loves me. He who loves me will be loved by my Father, and I too will love him and show myself to him.[251]

Jesus reveals Himself to us as the Holy Spirit.

Jesus, when here as a man, told us:

→ Not everyone who says to me "Lord, Lord," will enter the kingdom of heaven, but only he who does the will of my Father who is in heaven. Many will say to me on that day [Judgement Day, Last Day], "Lord, Lord, did we not prophesy in your name, and in your name drive out demons and perform many miracles?" Then I will tell them plainly, "I never knew you. Away from me you evildoers!"[252]

---

248 Bible, Matthew 5:17,18
249 Bible, Matthew 7:12
250 Bible, James 1:5
251 Bible, John 14:21
252 Bible, Matthew 7:21,22,23

God loves people. Yes He hates the evil that they sometimes do, but in the Bible, Paul, quoting the Old Testament, wrote:

→ Do not take revenge, my friends, but leave room for God's wrath, for it is written: "It is mine to avenge; I will repay," says the Lord [Deuteronomy 32:35]. "If your enemy is hungry, feed him; if he is thirsty, give him something to drink. In doing this, you will heap burning coals on his head." [Proverbs 25:21,22] Do not be overcome by evil, but overcome evil with good.[253]

God's love draws us near to Him. Muhammad's ideas of fighting to force religious belief are totally contrary to God's teaching found in the Scriptures.

In the introduction of Majid Fakhry's version of the Qur'an, he helps promote the idea of Christians having a corrupt book (the Bible)[254] based on two verses in the Qur'an:

• Woe unto those who write the Book with their hands, then say it is from Allah in order to sell it for a small price. There is a group of them who twist their tongues while reading the Book, so that you may suppose it is a part of the Book; whereas it is not a part of the Book. They also say: "It is from Allah," whereas it is not from Allah.[255]

The Bible is not corrupt, but his statement keeps Muslims from reading it; this prevents them from learning the truth. Majid Fakhry also states about the Qur'an:

• Due to the divergent readings of the sacred text and the danger of faulty oral transmission, a definitive edition was compiled in 651 AD...This edition has remained ever since as the authorized version of the Qur'an.[256]

---

253 Bible, Romans 12:19,20
254 Qur'an, Introduction, page 3, first paragraph, first sentence
255 Qur'an, 2:79 & 3:78
256 Qur'an, Introduction, page 2, first paragraph, second sentence

Who authorized it? Not God, and surely not Muhammad, he died in 632 A.D., nineteen years earlier. Any Muslim who still believes that the Bible has been corrupted as Muhammad has stated needs to ask himself three questions: What has been changed? Who did it? And, when did this take place? He will find no answers. Muslims need to be taught that it is not the Bible that is corrupt, but that it is the Qur'an that is corrupt.

→ Many false prophets will appear and deceive many people. False prophets will appear and perform great signs and miracles to deceive even the elect – if that were possible.[257]

Muhammad's Qur'an has misled many millions of people. But this book, the Qur'an, may never have been written if the concept of the "trinity" of God had not been created. This traditional teaching of the Church, the trinity, still taught today, is not only a stumbling block for those trying to find or serve God, but is indirectly responsible for the death of many.

---

257 Bible, Matthew 24:11,24

PART 3 - THE CHAOS THE TRINITY CREATED WITHIN CHRISTIANITY

When there is only one God, only one Jesus Christ, why do various "Christian" churches claim that only their particular group follows God's commandments? Are they not stumbling blocks to the rest of the world?

This concept of *three persons in one God*, the trinity of God, was instrumental in changing the understanding of who has the authority in the Church, Jesus, or the leaders of religious groups.

The next four chapters are going to compare the teaching of Jesus from Bible verses, to some of the teachings of Catholics, Mormons, Jehovah's Witnesses, and Oneness Pentecostals.

CHAPTER 1 - THE BIBLE VS. CATHOLICISM

Jesus said:

→ You are not to be called "Rabbi," for you have only one Master
and you are all brothers. And do not call anyone on earth "father,"
for you have one Father, and He is in heaven. Nor are you to be
called "teacher," for you have one Teacher, the Christ.[258]

Jesus, the Christ of the Scriptures, is the one in whom Christians trust
and to whom they pray. They take all their spiritual learning directly
from Him and the Bible. But, the Vatican II Council, concluded:

---

258 Bible, Matthew 23:8,9,10

- It is not from Sacred Scripture alone that the Church draws her certainty about everything which has been revealed. Both Sacred Scripture and Sacred Tradition are to be accepted and venerated with the same sense of loyalty and reverence.[259]

This "Sacred Tradition" they write of, results in the Pope's word becoming Catholic law. Here are four examples:

1. Their priests are called *fathers*, contrary to what Jesus taught. Catholics idolize the Pope when they call him the *Holy Father* even though Jesus said not to worship anyone but God. Jesus is our Father in heaven.

- → For to us a child is born, to us a son is given, and the government will be on his shoulders. And he will be called Wonderful Counselor, Mighty God, Everlasting Father, Prince of Peace.[260]

- → You are not to be called "Rabbi," for you have only one Master and you are all brothers. And do not call anyone on earth "father," for you have one Father, and he is in heaven. Nor are you to be called ""teacher," for you have one Teacher, the Christ.[261]

2. Catholics pray to Mary or their saints, and keep statues of her which is idolatry. Our record of Christ's teachings, the Bible, in Matthew 1:18 and Luke 1:31, 32, 33, 34, 35 tells us that the virgin, Mary, was made pregnant by the Holy Spirit – God. Mary's response:

- → I am the Lord's servant, may it be to me as you have said.[262]

The Immaculate Conception took place *within* Mary's womb, but the Roman Catholic Church teaches that Mary was born *of* an immaculate conception, supposedly without sin. This is contrary to the teaching found in Bible that only Jesus was sinless. God made Mary pregnant.

259 *The New American Bible, Saint Joseph Edition*, Published by Catholic book publishing Co. *Dogmatic Constitution on Divine Revelation*, Part 2, paragraph #9

260 Bible, Isaiah 9:6

261 Bible, Matthew 23:8,9,10

262 Bible, Luke 1:38

He used Mary to come into the world as the man Jesus. Mary was only the mother of Jesus the human, not Jesus who is Spirit. She is not the "Mother of God." God, who is Spirit, became flesh – Jesus.

> → ...the Word [Jesus] was God. The Word became flesh and lived for a while among us.[263]

Over 1500 years before the Roman Catholic Church was started, God gave us Ten Commandments. In the Bible (Exodus 20:4) God said that we were not to make idols, nor to worship them, and yet the Catholic Church keeps statues of Mary and prays to her. How did they get away with this: by changing the Ten Commandments that God gave to us through Moses.

The Roman Catholic Church, when including the Ten Commandments in its *Catechism of the Catholic Church* – CCC[264] ignores the second commandment relating to idolatry, and splits the tenth commandment into two. In the Bible the second one states:

> → You shall not make for yourselves an idol in the form of anything in heaven above or on the earth below. You shall not bow to them or worship them...[265]

And God's tenth commandment tells us:

> → You shall not covet your neighbor's house. You shall not covet your neighbor's wife, nor his manservant or maidservant, his ox or donkey, or anything that belongs to your neighbor.[266]

But the Roman Catholic Church replaced the second commandment by making coveting your neighbor's wife the ninth commandment and coveting your neighbor's goods as the tenth commandment.

---

263 Bible, John 1:1,14
264 *Catechism of the Catholic Church,* Published by Doubleday, ISBN - 0385479670
265 Bible, Exodus 20:4
266 Bible, Exodus 20:17

This catechism calls Mary the "Holy Mother of God"[267] and that she is a:

- "preeminent and wholly unique member of the Church, the Church's model of faith and charity"[268]

However, Jesus states in the Bible that only God is holy. Jesus is our example, not Mary.

Jesus is the only person to whom we should pray, He said:

→ When you pray, go into your room, close the door and pray to your Father, who is unseen. Then your Father, who sees what is done in secret, will reward you.[269]

→ This is how you should pray: "Our Father in heaven…"[270]

→ You may ask me for anything in my name, and I will do it.[271]

Jesus is called:

→ Everlasting Father[272]

And Jesus' apostle Paul wrote these verses:

→ …there is one mediator between God and men, the man Christ Jesus.[273]

→ Everyone who calls on the name of the Lord, will be saved.[274]

---

267 *CCC*, 975
268 *CCC*, 967
269 Bible, Matthew 6:6
270 Bible, Matthew 6:9
271 Bible, John 14:14
272 Bible, Isaiah, 9:6
273 Bible, Timothy 2:5
274 Bible, Romans 10:13

→ To the church of God...all those everywhere who call on the name of our Lord Jesus...[275]

The Holy Bible tells us that the Lord Jesus, while living as a man, had four brothers:

→ ...brothers James, Joseph, Simon and Judas [Jude is a form of Judas].[276]

In the Epistle of Jude, first verse, Jude writes:

→ Jude, a servant of Jesus Christ and a brother of James...[277]

Jude tells us to remember the words that the apostles of Jesus Christ spoke. He calls Jesus "our only Sovereign and Lord." Jude was a follower of Jesus, not someone to be prayed to.

Praying to Mary, Jude, or any other *saint* as Catholics are taught is contrary to what the Lord Jesus, who is God, teaches us. There is a danger in praying to any name other than that of Jesus; the Devil can answer.

→ Satan himself masquerades as an angel of light.[278]

Jesus told us:

→ Not everyone who says to me, "Lord, Lord," will enter the kingdom of heaven, but only he who does the will of my Father who is in heaven. Many will say to me on that day, "Lord, Lord, did we not prophesy in your name, and in your name drive out demons and perform many miracles?" Then I will tell them plainly, "I never knew you. Away from me you evildoers!"[279]

But, if we obey His commands He will show Himself to us (John 14:21).

---

275 Bible, 1 Corinthians 1:2
276 Bible, Matthew 13:55
277 Bible, Jude 1
278 Bible, 2 Corinthians 11:14
279 Bible, Matthew 7:21,22,23

3. Today, the Roman Catholic priests still cannot get married. Nowhere in the New Testament did either Jesus or His apostle Paul teach that anybody could not be married. Paul said that bishops could be married (Timothy 3:2). But the Roman Catholic *authorities* victimize their priests by not allowing them to have a wife; the results, too many Catholic priests have been found to be child molesters.

4. A real perversion in the Roman Catholic Church's "Sacred Tradition" is its concept that it promotes about the sacrifice of Jesus' life on the cross. They believe that their gift to God is Jesus. The definition of *Mass* that the Catholic Church gives us is the following:

- The Mass is the giving of a gift to God.[280]

This gift they presume to be giving is:

- The gift we give to God at Mass is the life of Christ Himself. At each Mass we re-offer to the Father the same gift that Christ offered on Calvary – His own life.[281]

What a horrible way to think of God's gift to us! The most venerated verse for Christians in the whole Bible is:

→ For God so loved the world that *He gave* His one and only Son that whoever believes in him shall not perish but have eternal life.[282]

God, in the form of the man Jesus, suffered and died on the cross to pay for our debt to God, our sins. Jesus' death on the cross was God's gift to us, not our gift to God.

H. H. Halley had good cause to write:

---

280 *The Catholic Missal*, Published by the Catholic Press, Copyright 1955
281 *The Catholic Missal*
282 Bible, John 3:16

- "The Papacy is not a Church, but a political machine that got control of the Church, and by assumed prerogatives, interposed itself between God and God's people."[283]

In other words, it thinks of itself as mediators between God and men. But:

→ there is one mediator between God and men, the man Christ Jesus.[284]

The "Sacred Traditions," or teachings, of the Catholic Church are stumbling blocks to those who follow this organization. How will these people find and have a relationship with Jesus, our God, when they are taught to pray to Mary, and to look to the Pope for guidance?

---

283 H.H. Halley, Halley's Bible Handbook, 24th edition, Published by Zondervan Publishing House, page 784, ISBN - 0310257204

284 Bible, 1 Timothy 2:5

CHAPTER 2 - THE BIBLE VS. MORMONISM

Christians follow the teachings of Jesus and His twelve apostles, which are found in the Bible. Mormons follow the teachings of Joseph Smith, which are found in his two books: *The Book of Mormon* and *Doctrine and Covenants* (both published by The Church of Jesus Christ of Latter-day Saints). Joseph Smith claimed that Jesus said:

- I am the Father and the Son.[285]

---

285 *Book of Mormon*, Published by The Church of Jesus Christ of Latter-day Saints, Ether 3:14

He also said that not only did he see both Father and Son at the same time[286] but that:

- The Father has a body of flesh and bones as tangible as man's; the Son also; but the Holy Ghost has not a body of flesh and bones, but is a personage of Spirit.[287]

But in the Bible, Jesus said:

→ God is Spirit, and His worshipers must worship in spirit and in truth.[288]

And Jesus' apostle John wrote:

→ ...the Word was God. The Word became flesh and lived for a while among us.[289] (John 1:1,14)

Seven hundred years earlier, Isaiah wrote:

→ For to us a child is born, to us a son is given, and the government will be on his shoulders. And he will be called Wonderful Counselor, Mighty God, Everlasting Father, Prince of Peace.[290]

This tells us that God, who is Spirit, came to the earth in the form of a man – Jesus. God is one. So Joseph Smith's claim of seeing both Father and Son at the same time, and that *they* had "a body of flesh and bones as tangible as man's," is false. The teaching of the *trinity* of God gave the creator of Mormonism a confused concept of God. Because God is not a trinity, what Joseph Smith saw was not of God.

In the Bible, through His apostles, Jesus tells us that those who follow Christ are no longer under law but live by love (Romans 3:21, 22; 7:6;

---

286 *Doctrine and Covenants*, Published by The Church Of Jesus Christ of Latter-day Saints, Joseph Smith, History 1:17

287 *Doctrine and Covenants*, 130:22

288 Bible, John 4:24

289 Bible, John 1:1,14

290 Bible, Isaiah 9:6

10:4; 13:9; 13:10; and Galatians 2:16, 19; 3:10, 11, 25; 5:4, 18. There is greater detail of these verses in Part 4, chapter 1).

Jesus gave two commands: love the Lord and love your neighbor. He said:

→ All the Law and the Prophets hang on these two commandments.[291]

Jesus' apostle Paul said:

→ The entire law is summed up in a single command, "Love your neighbor as yourself."[292]

But, Mormons are taught that they must learn to obey many commands.[293] Contained in the book *Doctrine and Covenants* is the Mormon tenet, *The Articles of Faith*. The third article states:

• ...all mankind may be saved by the obedience to the laws and ordinances of the Gospel.[294]

The word Gospel has nothing to do with *obeying laws and ordinances*. The word Gospel (from the Old English godspell) translates the Greek euangelion (eu = good + angellein = to announce) – *good news*. The good news is that Jesus came to set us free from the law by paying for our sins, with His life. He died for us. Jesus teaches us to live by God's law of love, not by a written code of rules.

Christians are taught by God that once a man dies he faces judgment (Hebrews 9:27) and that we are to have nothing to do with the dead. From the Bible:

→ Let no one be found among you who practices divination or sorcery, interprets omens, engages in witchcraft, or casts spells,

---

291 Bible, Matthew 22:40
292 Bible, Galatians 5:14
293 *Commands and Promises of God*, by President Spencer Kimball, Deseret publications, 1983
294 *Doctrine and Covenants*, The Articles of Faith

or who is a medium or spiritist or who consults the dead. Anyone who does these things is detestable to the Lord.[295]

Also, Jesus' apostle Paul tells us twice to avoid genealogies (1 Timothy 1:3, 4 and Titus 3:9).

But, Mormons are taught to study their genealogies and are baptized for the dead. They misunderstand the verse in 1 Corinthians 15:29 about being baptized for the dead. The *dead* in Paul's teaching here was none other than Jesus. If there wasn't a resurrection, why would someone be baptized in a *dead* person's name – that of Jesus? Jesus is alive and we are to have nothing to do with the dead.

In the Bible, Jesus' apostle Paul tells us that a man can have only one wife.[296] Joseph Smith also wrote two verses that say a man can have only one wife.[297] This agrees with the Bible, however, he contradicts himself in his book *Doctrine and Covenants* where he wrote that a man could have more than one wife at the same time.[298]

From the *Book of Mormon*, introduction:

- By the same power that Jesus Christ is the Savior of the world, Joseph Smith is his revelator and prophet in these last days.

Joseph Smith was a self-proclaimed prophet just like Muhammad. The Bible tells us:

→ There is one God and one mediator between God and man, the man Christ Jesus.[299]

Jesus (who comes as the Holy Spirit in us, if, and when we ask Him) is our one and only Teacher or *revelator* (Matthew 23:10).

---

295 Bible, Deuteronomy, 18:10, 11, 12
296 Bible, 1 Timothy 3:12 & Titus 1:6
297 *Book of Mormon*, Jacob 2:27 & 3:5
298 *Doctrine and Covenants*, 132:61
299 Bible, 1 Timothy 2:5

→ Nor are you to be called "teacher," for you have one Teacher, the Christ.[300]

Jesus told us:

→ Many false prophets will appear and deceive many people. False prophets will appear and perform great signs and miracles to deceive even the elect – if that were possible.[301]

Joseph Smith, even though stealing from the Bible, couldn't keep his story straight. He was a false prophet. This false prophet created the Book of Mormon; therefore, the Book of Mormon is false. Mormons do not teach the truth about Jesus.

Jesus is the only person to whom we should pray, and if we obey His commands He will show Himself to us (John 14:21). The Bible tells us:

→ Every one who calls on the name of the Lord [Jesus] will be saved.[302]

Jesus told us:

→ Not everyone who says to me "Lord, Lord," will enter the kingdom of heaven, but only he who does the will of my Father who is in heaven. Many will say to me on that day, "Lord, Lord, did we not prophesy in your name, and in your name drive out demons and perform many miracles?" Then I will tell them plainly, "I never knew you. Away from me you evildoers!"[303]

Just as Muhammad of the Qur'an stated that the Bible had been corrupted, so too does the *Articles of Faith* in the Mormon religion give the idea that there are problems with the Bible. The Mormon *Articles of Faith* #8 states:

---

300 Bible, Matthew 23:10
301 Bible, Matthew 24:11, 24
302 Bible, Romans 10:13
303 Bible, Matthew 7:21, 22, 23

- We believe the Bible to be the word of God as far as it is translated correctly; we also believe the Book of Mormon to be the word of God.[304]

How does the Mormon Church accept the statement "as far as it is translated correctly" and not apply it to Joseph Smith's *Book of Mormon*? (The story in the *Book of Mormon* has Joseph Smith translating the book from some ancient gold plates that do not exist.)

Joseph Smith's book, *The Book of Mormon*, is a stumbling block, and the Mormon Church perpetuates its false teaching. They are stumbling blocks to many around the world because they go door-to-door teaching this false belief, preventing others from learning the truth about Jesus.

---

304 Doctrine and Covenants, The Articles of Faith #8

CHAPTER 3 - THE BIBLE VS. JEHOVAH'S WITNESSES

Another group that goes door-to-door teaching false ideas about Jesus is the Jehovah's Witnesses. In this next chapter we will see that they too are a part of this chaos. Christians follow the teachings of Jesus and His apostles found in the Bible. Jesus said:

→ I am the way and the truth and the life.[305]

The Jehovah's Witness does not believe in the *trinity*, but the trinity concept has driven him to accept the changes in the Bible that the *Watch Tower Society* has made. This organization (started by Charles Taze Russell, 1852–1916) created and published a book called *The*

---

305 Bible, John 14:6

Kingdom Interlinear Translation of the Greek Scriptures (Published 1969, by Watch Tower and Bible and Tract Society).

The Watch Tower Society used the *Westcott and Hort Greek text* as a basis of their transliteration. When they then translated it to English they change some words and left certain words out. They changed the book to fit their beliefs rather than believing what was written. They used this book to create their version of the Bible, *The New World Translation of the Holy Scriptures* (Copyright 1984, and published, by the Watch Tower Bible and Tract Society).

In the Bible, and in the Watch Tower Bible and Tract Society's version of the Bible, are found the verses: Isaiah 44:6; Isaiah 43:10; Corinthians 8:6; Ephesians 4:6. All these verses state that there is only one God.

Because they could not make sense of the supposed *trinity*, the Watchtower Society changed their version of John 1:1 from "the Word was God" to "the Word was *a* god" making Jesus to be another god instead of being the one and only God. They changed the Bible to fit their understanding and created a false doctrine. Jehovah's Witnesses do not follow the teachings of Jesus. They follow the teachings of the Watch Tower Bible and Tract Society.

The Watch Tower Society changed the word *Lord* to *Jehovah* (Yahweh) in Romans 10:13:

- Everyone who calls on the name of *Jehovah* will be saved.[306]

But the original stated:

→ Everyone who calls on the name of the Lord will be saved.[307]

The Society has even gone as far as calling God *it* when they refer to the Holy Spirit (Romans 8:27, Galatians 4:6, and 1 Corinthians 12:11) and state that this *it* is:

---

306 *New World Translation of the Holy Scriptures*, Copyright 1984 by Watch Tower Bible and Tract Society of Pennsylvania, Romans 10:13

307 Bible, Romans 10:13

- God's active force, not a person.[308]

An active force cannot not speak, changing words, changes meanings. The Bible states:

→ The Holy Spirit [Jesus] said, "Set apart for me Barnabas and Saul for the work to which I have called them."[309]

The name Yahweh means *I am*. The English name Jesus from the Hebrew Je-shua means: Yah-saves/I am – saves (Yah is a contraction for Yahweh/Jehovah). Calling God Jesus, Yah-saves/Yahweh-is-salvation, honors the payment for our sins (by His death on the cross) that God has made for us when He came to the earth as a man.

If the Bible tells us that Jesus (I am – saves) is our one and only Lord (1 Corinthians 8:6, Ephesians 4:5), and that the Lord is the Spirit (Corinthians 3:17), then to call on the name Yahweh (I am) would be ignoring His gift of salvation – His death for us; to call the Lord Jesus, who is the Spirit, an *it*, would be reducing Him to a thing, rather than the person He is. Jesus warned us:

→ So I tell you, every sin and blasphemy will be forgiven men, but the blasphemy against the Spirit will not be forgiven. Anyone who speaks a word against the Son of Man will be forgiven, but anyone who speaks against the Holy Spirit will not be forgiven, either in this age or in the age to come.[310]

Any Jehovah's Witness who wants to be saved should leave the Watch Tower Organization and ask Jesus for forgiveness while they still can.

The Holy Spirit is not a power, an active force, or a thing. He is Yahweh (I – am) whom we call Jesus (I – am – saves). We call Him Jesus because He paid for our sins by dying on the cross for us. He comes to live in us if we ask Him to do so.

---

308 *New World Translation of the Holy Scriptures*, Bible topics for discussion, 41 Spirit, Spiritism, A, Page 1658

309 Bible, Acts 13:2

310 Bible, Matthew 12:31,32

Jesus, our God and Savior, is the only person to whom we should pray, and if we obey His commands He will show Himself to us. Jesus said:

→ Whoever has my commands and obeys them, he is the one who loves me. He who loves me will be loved by my Father, and I too will love him and show myself to him.[311]

In the Watch Tower Society's version of the Bible, in this above verse, it is written more emphatically:

• …I will love him and *plainly* show myself to him.[312]

But the Jehovah's Witness is purposely misdirected by the removal of the word *me* in the verse John 14:14. From the Bible Jesus told us:

→ You may ask *me* for anything in my name, and I will do it.[313]

The Kingdom Interlinear Translation of the Greek Scriptures, a book published by The Watch Tower Society published in 1969, has the word *me* in the verse John 14:14. But when the *New World Translation of the Holy Scriptures* was published, the Society deliberately left the word *me* out of the verse John 14:14. Their version states:

• If you ask anything in my name I will do it.[314]

Jesus, when here as a man, told us:

→ Not everyone who says to me "Lord, Lord," will enter the kingdom of heaven, but only he who does the will of my Father who is in heaven. Many will say to me on that day, "Lord, Lord, did we not prophesy in your name, and in your name drive out demons and perform many miracles?" Then I will tell them plainly, "I never knew you. Away from me you evildoers!"[315]

---

311 Bible, John 14:21
312 New World Translation of the Holy Scriptures, John 14:21
313 Bible, John 14:14
314 *New World Translation of the Holy Scriptures*, John 14:14
315 Bible, Matthew 7:21, 22, 23

→ Everyone who calls on the name of the Lord [Jesus is Lord] will be saved.[316]

Any teaching that diverts our knowledge of the truth of God is a problem. Like many other religious groups, Jehovah's Witnesses believe that they are spreading the truth. But unless they tell the truth about Jesus, they are only spreading confusion, more chaos.

The Jehovah's Witness' religious beliefs about blood transfusions conflict with the Bible, and, the laws of the land. Their refusal to permit blood transfusions is based on an incorrect understanding of these two verses in the Bible:

→ It is my judgment, therefore, that we should not make it difficult for the Gentiles who are turning to God. Instead, we should write to them, telling them to abstain from food polluted by idols, from sexual immorality, from the meat of strangled animals and from blood.[317]

→ As for the Gentile believers, we have written to them our decision that they should abstain from food sacrificed to idols, from blood, from the meat of strangled animals and from sexual immorality.[318]

There are no other verses in the New Testament that refer to abstinence from blood. These verses from the book of Acts were based on God's law from the Old Testament. Here are some examples:

→ This is a lasting ordinance for the generations to come, wherever you live: You must not eat any fat or any blood.[319]

→ And wherever you live, you must not eat the blood of any bird or animal.[320]

---

316 Bible, Romans 10:13
317 Bible, Acts 15:19,20
318 Bible, Acts 21:25
319 Bible, Leviticus 3:17
320 Bible, Leviticus 7:26

→ Do not eat any meat with the blood still in it.[321]

→ You must not eat the blood. Be sure you do not eat the blood, because the blood is the life, and you must not eat the life with the meat.[322]

→ Do not sin against the Lord by eating meat with blood still in it.[323]

It is easy to understand that the writer or speaker in the New Testament is referring to the Old Testament's statements about the *eating* of blood. No one even knew of blood transfusions in those days.

Jesus said that the two most important commandments of God were to love God, and love your neighbor. If my neighbor is going to die because of a lack of blood, then isn't it an act of love to sacrifice some of my blood to keep them alive?

Our laws allow religious freedom. When that freedom contradicts not only our laws, but God's law of love, then that religious freedom is abuse. It is only used as a method for controlling others.

321 Bible, Leviticus 19:26
322 Bible, Deuteronomy 12:16, 23
323 Bible, 1 Samuel 14:34

CHAPTER 4 - THE BIBLE VS. ONENESS PENTECOSTALS

Although Oneness Pentecostals claim that God is one, not three in one, the trinity, that is not what they teach. David K. Bernard in his book *The Oneness of God*[324] writes:

- Jesus Christ had two distinct natures. One nature is human or fleshly, the other is divine or spirit.[325]

If the meaning of the word *distinct* is: *recognizably not the same, clearly different*; and the meaning of the word *natures* is: *the basic character or*

---

324   David K, Bernard, *The Oneness of God*, Published 2011 by Word Aflame Press, ISBN - 9781567222203

325   *The Oneness of God*, The Dual Nature of Christ, chapter 5

disposition of a person (*Funk and Wagnals Standard College Dictionary*, 1989 edition), then David K. Bernard is still thinking of two persons – binitarian.

God is Spirit, and His character or disposition is Holy. He took on flesh, He did not change His character or disposition. The Bible tells us:

→ ...the Word was God.[326]

→ The Word became flesh and lived a while among us.[327]

There is a need for more dictionary definitions here:

Being – *a living thing, existence, as opposed to nonexistence*;

Person – *any human being* [God is the Supreme Being] *considered as a distinct entity or personality; an individual*;

Personality – *distinctive qualities or characteristics of a person.*

Mr. Bernard wrote of God having personality. But then in chapter twelve he wrote:

• Speaking of God as a person does not do justice to Him. The word person connotes a human being with a human personality – an individual with body, soul, and spirit. Thus, we limit our conception of God if we describe Him as a person. For this reason, this book has never said there is one person in the Godhead or God is one person. The most we have said is that Jesus Christ is one person, because Jesus was God manifested in flesh as a human person. The Son is begotten, not eternal. The Son of God came into actual existence at the incarnation.[328]

Again, we can see he is thinking of two different persons when he writes: He separates Jesus from God. God, who is Spirit, has always

---

326 Bible, John 1:1

327 Bible, John 1:14

328 The Oneness of God, chapter 12

existed, but He manifested Himself as the man Jesus with all the limitations of a man. Because the man Jesus was/is God, He could still calm the storm, heal the sick, perform miracles, and raise the dead. For Bernard to say that Jesus is not eternal separates Jesus from who He is – God. If in Bernard's mind, Jesus only came into existence at the incarnation, then how does he reconcile John 1:3 where John states that all things were created by Him – Jesus, the Word.

Gregory A. Boyd, who at one time belonged to the Oneness Pentecostal group, in refuting Oneness Pentecostals in his book *Oneness Pentecostals and The Trinity*[329] wrote:

- The analogy that has been most frequently employed for understanding the Trinity throughout church history has been one that likens the Trinity to the inner constitution of a single human person! This analogy is called the "psychological model" of the Trinity, for it is based on the psychology of a person.[330]

But he is not explaining God as a single entity here. He compares the *trinity* of God to *his* belief of a man's *plurality*. He writes:

- The unity of a self-conscious human person involves a genuine internal plurality. This internal relationality is manifested every time we think about or talk to ourselves.[331]

So if I talk to myself there is two of me? He goes on to state:

- Another version of this model suggests that the Father, Son, and Holy Spirit are something like the self's relationship to its own self-image.[332]

He completes these statements with:

---

329 *Oneness Pentecostals and The Trinity*, Published by Baker books, 1992, ISBN - 0801010195

330 *Oneness Pentecostals and The Trinity*, chapter 8

331 *Oneness Pentecostals and The Trinity*, chapter 8

332 *Oneness Pentecostals and The Trinity*, chapter 8

- The "fellowship" of the three divine "persons" is something like this, according to the model.[333]

Not only is this the same problem discussed earlier, man creating God in man's image, rather than God creating man in God's image, but he has further complicated any understanding by creating two *selves* in one man.

If the dictionary definition of the word *self* means: *anything considered as having a distinct personality*, or, *an individual known or considered as the subject of his own consciousness*, then according to Boyd, I am two persons. Trying to prove the trinity will always bring nonsensical explanations. Both Moses and Jesus stated that God is one, not three in one.

---

333 *Oneness Pentecostals and The Trinity*, chapter 8

PART 4- MORE CHAOS OR CONFUSION

CHAPTER 1 - THE LORD'S DAY

About the time the concept of trinity was created, another twist in the truth was perpetrated upon us – the day of the Sabbath, the Lord's Day. Jews look to the seventh day of the week, Muslims observe Friday, and most Christians take Sunday as the Lord's Day. This difference of opinion about which day is the right day has even divided the Christians. Jesus said:

> → Do not think that I have come to abolish the Law or the Prophets; I have not come to abolish them but to fulfill them. I tell you the truth, until heaven and earth disappear, not the smallest letter, not the least stroke of the pen, will by any means disappear from the Law until everything is accomplished.[334]

---

334 Bible, Matthew 5:17, 18

The Ten Commandments (from Exodus 20) that God gave Moses still stand (the Sabbath being the fourth one). Nowhere in the Bible does it say that God changed the Sabbath.

In the fourth century A.D., the Roman Emperor Constantine (the Roman Empire took over the Church to form the Roman Catholic Church) changed the Lord's Day from Saturday to Sunday so as to win sun worshipers (Sun-day) to Christ. He compromised the truth, and this tradition, passed on to us by the Roman Catholic Church, is still practiced to this day by the majority of Christian Churches. The Vatican of the Roman Catholic Church even admits it changed the day believing it had and has the authority to do so.

Evangelical Christians are wrong to promote Sunday as the Lord's Day. Seventh-Day Adventists are right in teaching that the Lord's Day – the Sabbath – is Saturday, not Sunday. But, although the Seventh-Day Adventist Church observes the correct day, there is a problem with how the Adventists present this information. The following statement is taken from the Seventh-day Adventist's official website (Adventist.ca/about/beliefs/):

- Seventh-day Adventists accept the Bible as their only creed and hold certain fundamental beliefs to be the teaching of the Holy Scriptures.[335]

Of their 28 fundamental beliefs, number 18 states:

- One of the gifts of the Holy Spirit is prophecy. This gift is an identifying mark of the remnant church and was manifested in the ministry of Ellen G. White. As the Lord's messenger, her writings are a continuing and authoritative source of truth which provide for the church comfort, guidance, instruction, and correction. They also make clear that the Bible is the standard by which all teaching and experience must be tested.[336]

---

335 Adventist.ca/about/beliefs/
336 Adventist.ca/about/beliefs/ #18

Ellen G. White (1827–1915) wrote *The Great Controversy*,[337] a book from which the Adventists have taken some of their teachings. Unfortunately, the Seventh-day Adventist Church did not test Ellen G. White's book. In it, White misquotes the Bible which proves that she was not a prophet, or, "the Lord's messenger." Chapter 40, paragraph 13, E. G. White writes:

- The enemies of God's law, from the ministers down to the least among them, have a new conception of truth and duty. Too late they see that the Sabbath of the fourth commandment is the seal of the living God.[338]

Henry Feyerabend, in his book *So Many Religions! Why?*[339] writes:

- Revelation 7 and Ezekiel 20 indicate that the seal or mark of God is the fourth commandment observance of the Sabbath.[340]

No doubt he learned this from White. But both of these statements are errors. Mr. Feyerabend states (page 209) that *sign* and *seal* are interchangeable in the Bible; they're not. The word that he is referring to in Ezekiel 20:12 was *sign*, not *seal*. The word *sign* in Ezekiel 20:12 translated from Hebrew means: *a signal, flag, or beacon*. The word *seal* in Revelation 7:2, translating from Greek, means: *to stamp, or mark*. This word *seal* in Revelation 7:2 translates the same Greek word used by the apostle Paul when he tells us:

- → Having believed [in Christ], you were marked in him with a seal, the promised Holy Spirit, who is a deposit guaranteeing our inheritance...[341]

---

337 Ellen G. White, *The Great Controversy*, Published by Pacific Press Associations, copyright originally 1888

338 The Great Controversy, chapter 40, 13th paragraph

339 Henry Feyerabend, *So Many Religions! Why?* Maracle Press Limited, a subsidiary of Pacific Publishing Association, 1991

340 *So Many Religions! Why?* page 208

341 Bible, Ephesians 1:13

→ He [God] anointed us, set his seal of ownership on us, and put his Spirit in our hearts as a deposit, guaranteeing what is to come.[342]

The word *seal* translates from the Greek, *mark or stamp*. The Holy Spirit of God, not the Sabbath, is the seal (mark or stamp) of God.

The seal is God himself as the Holy Spirit in born again (baptized in the Spirit) Christians. The seal has nothing to do with the Sabbath at all. The idea in the Adventist's teachings, that unless you keep the Sabbath you are doomed, is just another way of controlling people, keeping them separate from other Christians.

In chapter 27, paragraph 15, of her book, White writes that:

• The apostle James, who wrote after the death of Christ, refers to the Decalogue [the Ten Commandments] as the "royal law."[343]

She quotes this as coming from James 2:8. But the verse in the Bible, James 2:8, is written:

→ If you really keep the royal law found in Scripture, "Love your neighbor as yourself," you are doing right.[344]

This does not come from the Ten Commandments (so it has nothing to do with the Sabbath), but rather from various other laws written in the book of Leviticus (Leviticus19:18).

Chapter 27, paragraph 12, White wrote:

• One source of danger is the neglect of the pulpit to enforce the divine law.[345]

According to the Old Testament, anyone claiming to be a prophet for God must tell the truth 100% of the time, or they were to be put to

---

342 Bible, 2 Corinthians 1:21,22

343 *The Great Controversy*, chapter 27, paragraph 15

344 Bible, James 2:8

345 *The Great Controversy*, chapter 27, paragraph 12

death (Deuteronomy 13:1-5, 18:20). Wow, if that was enforced today she should have been put to death. When you "Love your neighbor as yourself" you serve, not enforce.

The Seventh-day Adventist's statement that the Bible is their only creed cannot be true since they take White's word as an "authoritative source of truth."

Another problem in the Seventh-day Adventist Church's beliefs is that when this church divides God's laws into 4 divisions: ceremonial, dietary, civil, and moral (they claim that the moral law is the Ten Commandments), it claims that the moral portion is not included when in Jesus' apostle Paul's writings, he tells us of no longer being under the law. When Paul states that we Christians are no longer under the law, he uses as an example the tenth commandment of the Ten Commandments: "Do not covet." (Romans 7:7) Paul does not discriminate between laws. Why then, does the Adventist Church separate the laws?

When Jesus gave these two commands – love the Lord and love your neighbor – He continued with these words:

→ *All the Law* and the Prophets hang on these two commandments.[346]

And in Galatians 5:14, Jesus' apostle Paul said:

→ *The entire law* is summed up in a single command, "Love your neighbor as yourself."[347]

The Bible tells us that God's Law still exists, and that God's Law will always exist for lawbreakers. But, the Bible also tells us that Christians (born again) are no longer under the law:

---

346 Bible, Matthew 22:40
347 Bible, Galatians 5:14

→ But now, by dying to what once bound us, we have been released from the law so that we serve in the new way of the Spirit, and not in the old way of the written code.[348]

→ Christ is the end of the law so that there may be righteousness for everyone who believes.[349]

→ ...know that a man is not justified by observing the law, but by faith in Jesus Christ. For through the law I died to the law so that I might live for God.[350]

→ All who rely on observing the law are under a curse, for it is written: "Cursed is everyone who does not continue to do everything written in the Book of the Law." Clearly no one is justified before God by the law, because, "The righteous will live by faith." So the law was put in charge to lead us to Christ that we might be justified by faith. Now that faith has come, we are no longer under the supervision of the law.[351]

→ You who are trying to be justified by law have been alienated from Christ; you have fallen away from grace. If you are led by the Spirit, you are not under the law.[352]

In his writing to fellow Christians, Jesus' apostle Paul states:

→ God made you alive with Christ. He forgave us all our sins, having canceled the written code, with its regulations, that was against us and that stood opposed to us; He took it away, nailing it to the cross. Therefore do not let anyone judge you by what you eat or drink, or with regard to a religious festival, a New Moon celebration or a *Sabbath* day. These are a shadow of the things that were to come; the reality, however, is found in Christ.[353]

---

348 Bible, Romans 7:6
349 Bible, Romans 10:4
350 Bible, Galatians 2:16, 19
351 Bible, Galatians 3:10, 11, 24,2 5
352 Bible, Galatians 5:4, 18
353 Bible, Colossians 2:13, 14, 16, 17

Jesus gave us two commands: love the Lord, and love your neighbor. He said:

→ In everything, do to others what you would have them do to you, for this sums up the Law and the Prophets.[354]

But Christians follow Church traditions and won't follow Jesus' apostle Paul's teaching on how to love your neighbor. Paul said:

→ Though I am free and I belong to no man, I make myself a slave to everyone, to win as many as possible. To the Jews I became like a Jew, to win the Jews. To those under the law I became like one under the law (though I myself am not under the law), so as to win those under the law.[355]

Even though free from the law, if Christians gathered together, not on the first day of the week as their tradition is, but on the last day of the week, the Sabbath (according to the fourth commandment of God's Ten Commandments); they would not have the appearance of being lawbreakers.

The Seventh-Day Adventist belief that they alone are the remnant church – *God's people* because they keep the Sabbath, is a misconception. Christians are not saved by observing the Sabbath; they are saved by faith in Jesus. The Seventh-Day Adventist teaching that they are the only true church because only they keep the Sabbath, is a stumbling block. Keeping the law (the Sabbath) is not the requirement for entrance to heaven. But, Christians who carry their tradition of gathering together on Sunday rather than Saturday are stumbling blocks to those who believe that they are under the law such as Jews, Muslims, and Adventists. We need to quit following our traditional teachings, and promote the truth found in the Bible, about the Lord Jesus our God and Savior.

---

354 Bible, Matthew 7:12
355 Bible, 1 Corinthians 9:19, 20

CHAPTER 2 - THE RAPTURE THEORY EXAMINED

This chapter has nothing to do with the trinity; it is included because, like the trinity's misleading of Christians, creating chaos, the differing doctrines of Christ's return have created a disunity of the Christian community.

The Bible tells us that Jesus is returning to gather the elect. Who are the elect? And, who are the chosen people of God?

In the book of Acts, 17:1–4, we find that Paul, the apostle to the Gentiles, is in Thessalonica where he led some Jews and a large number of Greeks to the Lord. Later, in a letter to them he wrote:

→ Brothers loved by God, we know that He has *chosen* you…[356]

And in a letter to the Colossians he wrote:

→ Here there is no Greek or Jew, circumcised or uncircumcised, barbarian, Scythian, slave or free, but Christ is all and is in all. Therefore, as God's *chosen* people…[357]

He tells Christians that they are God's chosen people, and in the book of Matthew we find this statement:

→ For then there will be great distress [KJV, "great tribulation"], unequaled from the beginning of the world until now – and never to be equaled again. If those days had not been cut short, no one would survive. But for the sake of the *elect* those days will be shortened.[358]

Chosen and elect, translate the same root in Greek. So Paul's words here are telling us that Christians are God's chosen people, the elect. He also wrote:

→ According to the Lord's own word we tell you that we who are still alive, who are left till the coming of the Lord, will certainly not precede those who have fallen asleep. For the Lord Himself will come down from the heaven, with a loud command, with the voice of the archangel and with the trumpet call of God, and the dead in Christ will rise first. After that, we who are still alive and are left will be caught up with them in the clouds to meet the Lord in the air. And so we will be with the Lord forever.[359]

The Lord's own word:

---

356 Bible, 1 Thessalonians 1:4
357 Bible, Colossians 3:11,12
358 Bible, Matthew 24:21, 22
359 Bible, 1 Thessalonians 4:15, 16, 17

> → And He will send His angels with a loud trumpet call, and they will gather His *elect* from the four winds, from one end of the heavens to the other.[360]

Although the Old Testament referred to the Jews as God's chosen people, the New Testament refers to Christians as the elect or chosen.

Jesus is coming back to collect His Church, but there has been a debate and a misunderstanding for many years about whether Christians would leave this earth before or after the Great Tribulation. The belief of a pre-tribulation rapture is based on the mistranslation of a verse in 2 Thessalonians 2:7. Here is the verse *transliterated* from the Greek found in *The Zondervan Parallel New Testament in Greek and English*.[361]

- For the mystery already operates of lawlessness; only the restraining just now until out of midst it comes.[362]

And here is the mistranslation:

> → For the secret power of lawlessness is already at work; but the one who now holds it back will continue to do so till he is taken out of the way.[363]

Why it is incorrect will be explained in the next few paragraphs.

This incorrect version of the verse gives us the understanding that there is *someone* restraining the power of lawlessness and that this person is being removed. Many Christians believe this to be the Holy Spirit and that when He is removed, we as Christians would go with Him because He lives in us, hence a pre-tribulation rapture. Reading the four previous verses will give us a better understanding of the subject matter of the verse in question.

---

360 Bible, Matthew 24:30,31

361 *The Zondervan Parallel New Testament in Greek and English*, copyright 1975, Published by The Zondervan Corporation, Library of Congress Catalog Number - 75 - 4148

362 *The Zondervan Parallel New Testament in Greek and English*, 2 Thessalonians 2:7

363 Bible, 2 Thessalonians 2:7

In verse three, Paul introduces us to the man of lawlessness – the Antichrist. In verse four he tells about what this man of lawlessness does to exalt himself. Verse five is a simple reminder that Paul has previously explained this. In verse six we have a key to understanding verse seven:

→ And now you know what [not who] is holding him back, so that he may be revealed at the proper time.[364]

This verse tells us only that some *thing*, not some *one*, is holding the man of lawlessness back, and "holding him back" means that when he is no longer restrained he would be able to move freely. Our subject matter that Paul is concerned with is the restraint of the man of lawlessness, not the Holy Spirit.

According to *The New Strong's Exhaustive Concordance of the Bible*,[365] in the New Testament the word *taken* is used sixty-eight times. The meaning of the word *taken*, in 2 Thessalonians 2:7, is different from all the rest. Its meaning: *cause to be, generate, become, come into being, or arise.*[366] The word *comes* has been incorrectly translated *taken*.

In English, the word *taken* would have someone doing the work of taking something or someone. But the Greek, in this verse, is giving us the understanding that it (the Antichrist or man of lawlessness) is coming of its/his own accord, when the restraining is over at the proper time. It does not tell us who or what is doing the restraining, only that when the restraining is over, "out of the midst it comes."

The word *way*, used 137 times in the New Testament, is only used in this verse (and one other) with the meaning *middle, among or midst* (Strong's, 3319). If this verse was referring to the Holy Spirit coming out of the midst or out from among, then it would have had to be Him leaving Christians, since He is not in the worldly people.

---

364 Bible, 2 Thessalonians 2:6

365 *The New Strong's Exhaustive Concordance Of The Bible*, Thomas Nelson Publishers, 1984, ISBN - 0-8407-5360-8

366 *The New Strong's Exhaustive Concordance Of The Bible*, taken -1096

Our English versions of the Bible have one being removed out of the way (from a power outside of itself) rather than one coming out (self-exerted) from among. This verse does not refer to a restrainer being removed, but rather, the one being restrained coming out of the midst.

This verse is not stating that the Holy Spirit is being taken out of the way, but that the Antichrist, when no longer being restrained, comes out. Jesus said:

→ For false Christs and false prophets will appear and perform great signs and miracles to deceive even the elect – if that were possible.[367]

This next statement is not necessarily the truth, it is just a question of mine. Is it not possible that the Antichrist, or man of lawlessness, would not want to be recognized for what he really is, so in other words, self-restraint?

Because some Christians believe God's wrath and the great tribulation are one and the same, here are the definitions of these two words:

From Funk and Wagnalls Standard College Dictionary:

Tribulation – *A condition of affliction and distress, suffering.*

Wrath – *Extreme or violent rage or fury; vehement indignation, anger.*[368]

And from Strong's Concordance:

Tribulation: 2347 – *Pressure, trouble, persecution.*

Wrath: 2372 – *Fierceness, indignation;* 3709: *Violent passion, anger, vengeance.*[369]

---

367 Bible, Matthew 24:24

368 *Funk & Wagnalls Standard College Dictionary, Harper and Row Publishers,* 1989, ISBN - 0-88902-923-7

369 *The New Strong's Exhaustive Concordance Of The Bible,* tribulation - 2347, wrath - 2372, 3709

The *great tribulation* (Matthew 24: the whole chapter) is a time of trouble that all (alive at that time) are going to go through. After that, when Jesus returns to take us Christians away, then will come His wrath upon the rest of the world.

The elect, we Christians, are going through the tribulation. As a result of Christians being taught that they are not going through the tribulation, many will be disillusioned by the times of hardship. They are going to turn away from faith.

→ Then you will be handed over to be persecuted and put to death, and you will be hated by all nations because of me. At that time many will turn away from the faith and will betray and hate each other and many false prophets will appear and deceive many people. Because of the increase of wickedness, the love of most will grow cold, but he who stands firm to the end will be saved.[370]

→ After this I looked and there before me was a great multitude that no one could count, from every nation, tribe, people and language [not just Jews as some think], standing before the throne and in front of the Lamb. These are they who have come out of the great tribulation.[371]

Nowhere in the Bible does it say that there is a rapture of Christians before Jesus returns. The only rapture is at the Second Coming of Jesus when He will take us away.

→ They will see the Son of Man coming on the clouds of the sky, with power and great glory. And he will send his angels with a loud trumpet call, and they will gather his elect from the four winds, from one end of the heavens to the other.[372]

These will be all those who have a personal relationship with Jesus.

---

370   Bible, Matthew 24:9, 10, 11, 12, 13

371   Bible, Revelation 7:9, 14

372   Bible, Matthew 24:30, 31

Christians are the elect, or chosen, and will go through the Great Tribulation. Because of the sad condition of today's Church, there is a real necessity that the Church does go through this time of great distress. But far too many Christians, believing in a pre-tribulation rapture, believing they are not going to go through any time of great suffering, will not be ready for the times of trouble ahead. They will lose faith and fall away.

Religious freedom is changing. Soon, Christians will be forced to accept homosexuality in their churches or face persecution. Our countries have passed same-sex marriage laws, and already there are Christians being taken to court for standing up for the truth about homosexuality. How long will it be before ministers are not allowed to speak the truth from the Bible?

And is not the Islamic terrorist a form of persecution? The problem of terrorism is only going to grow in the near future.

How can Christians be ready for persecution when they think that they are going to leave this world before persecution comes? It won't come announced. It will suddenly be in our neighborhoods.

PART 5 - SUMMARY

CHAPTER 1 - ISLAMIC TERRORISM

It is no wonder, with the instructions of the Qur'an, that the Arab Muslims fight the Jews in Israel, and that the terrorist groups bomb the "Christian" West.

Even though our North American countries give us the freedom to believe in the religion of our choice, this should not allow us to propagate hate literature. When anyone uses the Qur'an to teach others about God, they are using a book that promotes hatred and violence towards Christians and Jews to the point of genocide.

The Canadian Criminal Code in section 318 (1 and 2) states:

1 – Everyone who advocates or promotes genocide is guilty of an indictable offense and liable to imprisonment for a term not exceeding five years.

2 – In this section "genocide" means any of the following acts committed with intent to destroy in whole or part any identifiable group, namely,

(a) killing members of the group; or

(b) deliberately inflicting on the group conditions of life calculated to bring about its physical destruction.

Genocide is against the law in both the United States and in Canada. According to Canadian law, the use of the Qur'an should be illegal.

CHAPTER 2 - CATHOLICISM

Catholic Answers, Inc. claims it is the largest Catholic apologetics and evangelization organization in North America. In its little booklet *Pillar of fire Pillar of truth*,[373] this organization claims that the Catholic Church is:

- The only true universal Christian Church that has existed since the time of Jesus.[374]

Under the Subtitle *The Magisterium (CCC 85, 888-892)*, the booklet states that the pope and the bishops form the teaching authority of the Church and are called the *magisterium* (teachers).[375] CCC 85 states:

---

373 *Pillar of fire Pillar of truth*, 1997, published by Catholic Answers, Inc.

374 *Pillar of fire Pillar of truth*, page 2

375 *Pillar of fire Pillar of truth*, page 12

- The task of giving an authentic interpretation of the Word of God, whether in its written form or in the form of Tradition, has been entrusted to the living, teaching office of the Church alone. This means that the task of interpretation has been entrusted to the bishops in communion with the successor of Peter, the Bishop of Rome.[376]

This Catholic organization states in its booklet that:

- An official interpreter is absolutely necessary if we are to understand the Bible properly.[377]

- The magisterium is infallible when it teaches.[378]

This not only contradicts Jesus' apostle John's statement:

→ ...the anointing you received from him [Jesus] remains in you, and you do not need anyone to teach you.[379]

It also contradicts Paul's statement:

→ There is one God and one mediator between God and men, the man Christ Jesus.[380]

"The magisterium is infallible when it teaches." How preposterous, do they think that they are gods? Even their own book reveals their errors:

- Yet this Magisterium is not superior to the Word of God, but is its servant.[381]

---

376 *CCC*, Part 1, chapter 2, article 2, 85
377 *Pillar of fire Pillar of truth*, page 12
378 *Pillar of fire Pillar of truth*, page 13
379 Bible, 1 John 2:27
380 Bible, 1 Timothy 2:5
381 *CCC*, Part 1, chapter 2, article 2, 86

History shows that the Roman Catholic Church is the remains of a takeover of the Church by the Roman Empire. In his book *Halley's Bible Handbook*,[382] Henry H. Halley states:

- The papacy is not a church, but a political machine that got control of the Church, and, by assumed prerogatives, interposed itself between God and God's people.[383]

- Emperor Theodosius (AD 378–395) made Christianity the state religion of the Roman Empire, and made church membership compulsory. The Church changed its nature, and had become a political organization.[384]

Through a succession of popes this takeover eventually brought about the Dark Ages, and today the Roman Catholic Church, the Vatican, still tries to assert authority over Jesus' Church.

The Roman Catholic Church's real motive, just like Muhammad of the Muslims, Joseph Smith of the Mormons, and Charles Russel of the Jehovahs Witnesses, is the attempt to usurp the authority of God/Jesus.

The Pope, according to the Roman Catholic Church, is the head of the body of believers, the Church; but the Bible states that Jesus is the head of His Church (Colossians 1:18, Ephesians 5:23).

The Roman Catholic Church wants to claim responsibility for being the only true Church. But what it is truly responsible for is creating the doctrine of the trinity in 381 A.D., and in so doing, being indirectly responsible for the creation of the religion of Islam, a religion of hatred towards Christians and Jews.

The Roman Catholic Church, the largest "Christian" church in the world, is a huge stumbling block for people. It has set itself up as the mediator between man and God, declaring its *authority* over mankind.

---

382 Henry H. Halley, *Halley's Bible Handbook,* 24 Edition, 1962, Zondervan Publishing House, ISBN - 0-310-25720-4

383 *Halley's Bible Handbook*, Church History, page 754

384 *Halley's Bible Handbook*, Church History, page 760

It requires its adherents to follow its "Sacred Traditions" rather than teaching them to follow the teachings of Jesus found in the Bible.

The Bible says that Jesus is our teacher, our only teacher; our mediator, our only mediator; and that He, and only He, is our Father. The "Holy Father," the Pope, is neither holy, nor anybody's father.

CHAPTER 3 - CATHOLICISM'S PROTESTANT DAUGHTERS

Catholicism's Protestant Daughters: The Church of England, the Anglican Church, the Presbyterians, the Methodists, the Baptists, the Southern Baptists, the Pentecostals, the Lutherans, the United Church of Christ, the Evangelicals, the Fundamentalists, the what-evers. These names are actually just terms used to distinguish groups, a form of separation, the *I don't like what you teach, I'm going to start my own church* religions. It is Jesus' Church. We belong to Him and we are all brothers; we are supposed to accept one another and be in one accord as He accepted us. A united Christian voice in praise of our God would be a strong sign to the world, but what we have today is dissension. There are over 3,000 different "Christian" denominations in North America alone.

The Moral Majority Coalition, a right-wing Christian group, has as its opponent, the Christian Alliance, a left-leaning group: Christian, and I use word loosely here, infighting, political differences.

Rather than showing the love of Jesus to the world by example, these two groups show their desires to be in control of the political arena. Are they a "light to the world" or a stumbling block? Why would any outsider choose their god?

Many of our pastors and theologians are stumbling blocks. They have been set up in the Church as the *stars* of *Church society* with their sermons being the center of Church activity. They are busy being *teachers*, teaching all about the Book and doctrinal theories, instead of teaching people how they themselves can get to know Jesus better. The Church building is more of a lecture hall than it is a house of prayer.

The Bible tells us about Jesus; what Christians need to know is how to build a relationship with Him so that we can become more intimate with Him. (More on this in the Part 6.)

The Bible tells us that in the last days people will be lovers of themselves, not lovers of God (2 Timothy 3:1–9). It also tells us that Jesus posed a question to His disciples, one that He does not answer:

→ When the Son of Man comes [Christ's second coming], will He find faith on the earth?[385]

Many young people today are looking for standards by which to live. Moderate Muslim teachings have the appearance of a higher standard of moral code than the "Christian" West presents. Is it no wonder that some people born in North America are choosing Islam? And, some of them will become terrorists.

Several times in the past, God used a foreign nation to chastise His people. Perhaps the birth of Islam in the Dark Ages of Christianity was/is such a chastisement. Is it possible that we are bringing the Great Tribulation upon ourselves?

---

385   Bible, Luke 18:8

The Great Tribulation will be a stumbling block to many and they will turn from their faith.

CHAPTER 4 - DOOR-TO-DOOR SALESMEN: MORMONS AND JEHOVAHS WITNESSES

Going door to door to tell the world about God is not a bad thing in and of itself; it is a good thing to do, but, it is essential to tell the truth about God.

These two religions use the Bible in their beliefs to present Jesus as a god, rather than as God, the one and only God as the Bible states. The leaders of these two organizations control their followers by feeding them false information, thereby separating them from Christians and the truth of Jesus Christ.

PART 6 - CONCLUSION

CHAPTER 1 - MEETING JESUS

People grow up inheriting all sorts of religious doctrinal beliefs, but when these beliefs are compared, truth will prevail.

The only way to stop Muslim terrorism is by educating the public. Love is what people are really looking for, and that is what God/Jesus teaches us through the words of the Bible and His Spirit in us.

Christian leaders need to be informed of their common mistake and responsibility for the damage they have caused. These same leaders need to apologize publicly for teaching this mistake: to their own Governments who are trying to keep the peace; and especially to Muslims who have suffered for so long under false understandings.

The consequences of Christian leaders or governmental authorities ignoring the truth because of the fear of "losing face" or because of "the need/greed for the oil of Muslim countries," will be not only a continuing terrorism, but will also be indirectly promoting the onset of another and far greater World War. Ignoring the rise of Adolf Hitler resulted in World War II. If we ignore the growth of Islamic terrorism, a nuclear war will be the consequence. The terrorist is wholeheartedly doing what he believes that God has instructed him to do. Is not the onus upon us to help him learn the truth?

Meeting Jesus

If an alien, from some far-distant galaxy, stopped by this planet to give a short message to us earthlings, you can be guaranteed that not only would every news channel be paying attention, everyone on earth would want to know what the alien had to say.

God *stopped* by the earth to give a message to His people. He loves us. The Bible states that Jesus was seen by more than 500 people after His resurrection from the dead (1Corinthians 15:6). God's words are recorded in the Bible by some of these people who met Him.

The Bible tells us that there is only one mediator between God and men – the man Jesus. One has to learn to look, not at the form of the man, but to look through the veil or cloak of the physical body and to see into the heart or spirit of who He is. God revealed Himself to man, as a man.

The man Jesus, made a very amazing claim. He said:

→ I am the way and the truth and the life.[386]

No man can rest his faith on another man's word for the truth. To know the truth one has to ask the author of truth – Jesus/God.

→ If any of you lacks wisdom, he should ask God, who gives generously to all without finding fault, and it will be given to him.[387]

386 Bible, John 14:6
387 Bible, James 1:5

Jesus said:

→ You may ask me for anything in my name and I will do it.[388]
(John 14:14)

God is much more than some powerful being who created the universe. The nature of His character is absolutely awesome and inspiring. One can't help but adore Him and fall in love, fascinated by His compassion, His kindness, His joy, His peace, His gentleness, His care, and all this for us, if we would only pay attention.

He will not have us as puppets or slaves; He gave us a free will to choose whether we regard Him or ignore Him. Many ignore Him to their loss; and there are far too many false teachers and false religions either to confuse man or to overwhelm him into a state of apathy. It is man's ignorance of God that causes the world to be in the condition it is – tormented by man's inhumanity to man.

If you haven't met Jesus yet, you are in for the treat of your life. All the descriptive words in the Bible and in our vocabulary are not enough to tell about how wonderful He is. He is the one who gives us beautiful sunsets, children to love and cherish, laughter, the emotions of love, the joy of life, and wonder of wonders – a promise of eternal life with Him with His companionship. The world and its pleasures are nothing compared to time spent in intimacy with Him, not just for the future, but even today, as we spend time with Him, He fills us with joy, *if,* we follow His teaching and love Him.

To think that God allowed the creatures He made, men, to spit upon Him, to mock Him, to jam a crown of thorns on His Head, to nail Him to a cross, to watch Him slowly suffer and die, and, throughout the centuries, to ignore His gift to us (His payment for our sins). All this shows His tremendous grace and patience, in His teaching us about how much love He has for us.

But, according to what the Bible states about the future (the Great Tribulation and Judgement Day/The Last Day) and what we can see

---

388 Bible, John 14:14

in the news of today, this grace won't last much longer. Jesus is coming back for His Church, soon.

If you haven't met Jesus before He returns, remember, as a man He said:

→ Whoever has my commands and obeys them, he is the one who loves me. He who loves me will be loved by my Father, and I too will love him and show myself to him.[389]

To meet Jesus is both difficult, and at the same time, easy. The hard part is choosing to believe that He is God. The easy part is, just ask Him. The Bible tells us:

→ That if you confess with your mouth, "Jesus is Lord," and believe in your heart that God raised Him from the dead, you will be saved.[390]

→ Everyone who calls on the name of the Lord will be saved.[391]

Jesus said:

→ Greater love has no one than this, that one lay down his life for his friends.[392]

Jesus did just that when He died on the cross, paying for our sins.

God/Jesus, who is Spirit, is Love. He is our God, Counselor, Master, Teacher, King, Father, Savior, and our best friend. He is our real "soul mate." His desire is to have a loving relationship with us. What will you do about His love for you?

---

389 Bible, John 14:21
390 Bible, Romans 10:9
391 Bible, Romans 10:13
392 Bible, John 15:13

CHAPTER 2- BIBLE READING

The main reason we have such a variety of "Christian" denominations in the world is the lack of effort put into reading the Bible – God's word to us. The cause of this is the idea of a hierarchy, or, the "ruling class" of a Christian community, brought into Christianity. Far too often people are…well, looking up to, almost worshiping: their pastors; the theologians; and even Christian authors. This leaves the layman's faith resting on the pastor's or theologian's teachings rather than on the words of Jesus.

Instead of looking to Jesus as the Head of the Church, as the Bible tells us, most Christians look to their pastors, ministers, priests, theologians – those with *professional credentials* – as their leader, teacher, counselor, or shepherd; in other words, their authority figure. Jesus said:

→ Nor are you to be called "teacher" for you have one Teacher, the Christ.[393]

And Jesus' apostle John said:

→ ...the anointing you received from Him remains in you, and you do not need anyone to teach you.[394]

Some pastors are humble and do well, but there are those who are charismatic, that is, not truly gifted by God, but rather, they have a commanding presence and are natural orators. They take on the role of leader, teacher, and so on only because they have been taught to do so by tradition. Because of this, not enough people read the Bible for themselves.

For hundreds of years the popes and bishops of the Roman Catholic Church controlled the people and the result of this was the Dark Ages. The Protestant Reformation and the invention of the printing press brought to the common people the printed word of God. Anybody can know God as well as any other person simply by reading God's word, and by talking to Him – prayer.

There is a real need for Christians to read/study the Bible for themselves. But people find many reasons not to do so: television, movies, sports, video games, the Internet, and so on. Our minds are busy with nonessentials instead of taking time to learn about God.

The traditional teaching of the "trinity" would not be so widely accepted if more Christians read the Bible for themselves.

Only with more Bible reading will the Christian community learn to understand God. This will not only bring unity amongst ourselves, we would become a better example to the world.

If you have never studied the Bible before, be forewarned; if you start reading the Old Testament first (also called The Old Covenant,

393   Bible, Matthew 23:10
394   Bible, John 2:27

the laws that Jews still live under today), you may get bogged down with too much information that isn't as relevant to us today as is the New Testament (New Covenant – new contract). Much of the Old Testament is history leading up to why Jesus came, whereas most of the New Testament is about Jesus, our relationship with Him, and with each other. The New Testament proclaims the law of Christ – love.

CHAPTER 3 - PRAYER

→ His divine power has given us everything we need for life and godliness through our knowledge of Him.[395]

Reading the Bible gives us intellectual knowledge; then when we pray, God turns the intellectual knowledge into spiritual knowledge. But there is a problem: we are mostly taught (usually by example) that prayer is *asking* of God, whether for others, or for ourselves.

The dictionary definition of the word *prayer* is twofold:

1 – *spiritual communion with God and awareness of His presence, as in adoring praise, thanksgiving, and confession of sins;*

---

395   Bible, 2 Peter 1:3

2 – *asking or requesting of God.*

We Christians spend more time looking for what we can get from God, rather than giving to Him our time in worship – thanking and praising Him for who He is, what He has done, and is now doing for us.

> → This is the confidence we have in approaching God: that if we ask anything according to His will, He hears us.[396]

God has given us insight on the best way to approach Him:

> → Enter His gates with thanksgiving and His courts with praise; give thanks to Him and praise His name.[397]

Paul also gives us understanding when he is talking about the gift of tongues:

> → If you are *praising* God with your spirit, how can one who finds himself among those who do not understand say "amen" to your *thanksgiving*, since he does not know what you are saying. You may be giving *thanks* well enough, but the other man is not edified.[398]

Start with thanks; remember "Enter His gates with thanksgiving." A heart of gratitude is a good attitude. Jesus died on the cross to pay for our sins, bringing us eternal life. Jesus has not only given us eternal life, He's given us a new and more abundant life to enjoy now, and the more we get to know Him, the more we enjoy His gift.

Intermingle praise with thanksgiving because we can thank God for His greatness, for all He has created, for His infinite knowledge and wisdom in caring for us, for His patience with us, for His grace towards us…the list is endless.

---

396   Bible, John 5:14
397   Bible, Psalm 100:4
398   Bible, 1 Corinthians 14:16, 17

Confess our sins. Starting with thanksgiving and praise helps us to understand the goodness and holiness of God, which in turn, reveals more of our sinful nature. Confessing our sins, asking for forgiveness, and believing that He does forgive us, helps us to understand better the depth of His love for us. When we ask God for something for ourselves (supplication) or for others (intercession), we can ask with selfish motives. However, the time spent thanking and praising God first, changes our hearts and minds so that we know what to ask.

Bible reading is fairly easy, it is learning to pray well that is difficult. If we can set a certain amount of time aside each day for prayer (even if just five minutes to start with) and every few days increase that time a little, we will begin to build our side of our relationship with the Lord Jesus. When we were first born in the flesh, we were helpless; we were fed and cared for. However, as we began to grow, we started to feed ourselves. It is the same when we are born in the spirit; God's joy carries us along until we are strong enough to feed our spirit through the tools He has given us to use. Just as the body needs both food and drink, so the spirit needs food (Scriptures) and drink (prayer). If one or the other were missing, we wouldn't grow. Strong muscles don't just happen; it takes exercise or work, through time, to develop them. Strong Christians don't just happen. Time spent praying alone with Jesus strengthens our relationship with Him.

→ When you pray, go into your room, close the door and pray to your Father, who is unseen. Then your Father, who sees what is done in secret, will reward you.[399]

→ Be joyful always; pray continually; giving thanks in all circumstances, for this is God's will for you in Christ Jesus.[400]

Jesus said:

---

399 Bible, Matthew 6:6
400 Bible, 1 Thessalonians 5:16, 17, 18

> → Remain in me and I will remain in you. No branch can bear fruit by itself; it must remain in the vine. Neither can you bear fruit unless you remain in me.[401]

Remaining in Jesus is being mindful of Him, constantly communicating with Him, and talking to Jesus about His attributes; about what He has created, why He created us, what He is promising us, who He is, His character, His love for us, and so on.

God, who is love, is always giving; and we, who want to be like Him, need to learn to give to Him. Spiritual dryness happens because we have wandered away from Him, thinking about ourselves instead of Him.

Why should God give us more if we don't learn to give in return? To enjoy more of God's Spirit we need to give more to Him; and since He created everything – including us – and has no needs, there is nothing we can give Him but our time in thanks and praise. And even of this, God has no need. Our giving of thanks and praise is for our good; it is we who need to learn to appreciate Him.

> → Through Jesus, therefore, let us continually offer to God a sacrifice of praise, the fruit of lips that confess His name.[402]

We are in error when we ask God to bring Spiritual revival; He has given that job to us.

> → I remind you to fan into flame the gift of God.[403]

It is up to us to stir up His gift in us, His love. The cure for Islamic terrorism and disunity in Christianity is the same, truth. Jesus is the truth, Jesus said:

> → I am the way and the truth and the life.[404]

---

401 Bible, John 15:4
402 Bible, Hebrews 13:15
403 Bible, 2 Timothy 1:6
404 Bible, John 14:6

APPENDIX

The Epistle Dedicatory of the King James Bible

(The following is written exactly as found in the beginning of a King James Bible. The words in italics are the key to the idea of the KJV being the "only correct" version.)

Part 1 – TO THE MOST HIGH and MIGHTY PRINCE JAMES by the Grace of God KING OF GREAT BRITAIN, FRANCE, and IRELAND, DEFENDER OF THE FAITH, & C. The Translators of this Bible wish Grace, Mercy, and Peace, through JESUS CHRIST our Lord.

Great and manifold were the blessings, most dread Sovereign, which Almighty God, the Father of all mercies, bestowed upon us the people of England, when first he sent Your Majesty's Royal Person to rule and reign over us. For whereas it was the expectation of many, who wished not well unto our Sion, that upon the setting of that bright Occidental Star, Queen Elizabeth of most happy memory, some thick and palpable clouds of darkness would so have overshadowed this Land, that men should have been in doubt which way they were to walk; and that it should hardly be known, who was to direct the unsettled State; the appearance of Your Majesty, as of the Sun in his strength, instantly dispelled those supposed and surmised mists, and gave unto all that were well affected exceeding cause of comfort; especially when we beheld the Government established in Your Highness, and Your hopeful Seed, by an undoubted Title, and this also accompanied with peace and tranquility at home and abroad.

But among all our joys, there was no one that more filled our hearts, than the blessed continuance of the preaching of God's sacred Word among us; which is that inestimable treasure, which excelleth all the riches of the earth; because the fruit thereof extendeth itself, not only to the time spent in this transitory world, but directeth and disposeth men unto that eternal happiness which is above in heaven.

Then not to suffer this to fall to the ground, but rather to take it up, and to continue it in that state, wherein the famous Predecessor of Your Highness did leave it: nay, to go forward with the confidence and resolution of a Man in maintaining the truth of Christ, and propagating it far and near, is that which hath so bound and firmly knit the hearts of all your Majesty's loyal and religious people unto You, that Your very name is precious among them; their eye doth behold You with comfort, and they bless You in their hearts, as that sanctified Person, who, under God, is the immediate Author of their true happiness. And this their contentment doth not diminish or decay, but every day increaseth and taketh strength, when they observe, that the zeal of Your Majesty toward the house of God doth not slack or go backward, but is more and more kindled, manifesting itself abroad in the farthest parts of Christendom, by writing in defense of the Truth (which hath given such a blow unto that man of sin, as will not be healed,), and every day at home, by religious and learned discourse, by frequenting the house of God, by hearing the Word preached, by cherishing the Teachers thereof, by caring for the Church, as a most tender and loving nursing Father.

There are infinite arguments of this right Christian and religious affection in Your Majesty; but none is more forcible to declare it to others than the vehement and perpetuated desire of accomplishing and publishing of this work, which now with all humility we present unto Your Majesty. For when Your Highness had once out of deep judgment apprehended how convenient it was, that out of the Original Sacred Tongues, together with comparing of the labours, both in our own, and other foreign Languages, of many worthy men who went before us, there should be one more exact Translation of the Holy Scriptures into the English Tongue; Your Majesty did never desist to urge and to excite those to whom it was commended, that the work might be hastened, and that the business might be expedited in so decent a manner, as a matter of such importance might justly require.

And now at last, by the mercy of God, and the continuance of our labours, it being brought unto such a conclusion, as that we have great hopes that the Church of England shall reap good fruit thereby;

we hold it our duty to offer it to Your Majesty, not only to our King and Sovereign, but as to the principal Mover and Author of the work: humbly craving of Your most Sacred Majesty, that since things of this quality have ever been subject to the censures of ill meaning and discontented persons, it may receive approbation and patronage from so learned and judicious a Prince as Your Highness is, whose allowance and acceptance of our labours shall more honour and encourage us, than all the calumniations and hard interpretations of other men shall dismay us. So that if on the one side, we shall be traduced by Popish Persons at home or abroad, who therefore will malign us, because we are poor instruments to make God's holy Truth to be yet more and more known unto the people, whom they desire still to keep in ignorance and darkness; or if, on the other side, we shall be maligned by self-conceited Brethren, who run their own ways, and give liking unto nothing, but what is framed by themselves, and hammered on their anvil; we may rest secure, supported within by the truth and innocency of a good conscience, having walked the ways of simplicity and integrity, as before the Lord; and sustained without by the powerful protection of Your Majesty's grace and favour, which will ever give countenance to honest and Christian endeavours against bitter censures and uncharitable imputations.

The Lord of heaven and earth bless Your Majesty with many and happy days, that, as his heavenly hand hath enriched Your Highness with many singular and extraordinary graces, so You may be the wonder of the world in this latter age for happiness and true felicity, to the honour of that great GOD, and the good of his Church, through Jesus Christ our Lord and only Savior.

Part 2 – Found in the front cover of an "Authorized" King James Version Bible: "All rights in respect of the Authorized King James Version of the Holy Bible are *vested* in the Crown in the United Kingdom and controlled by Royal Letters Patent. No part of this publication may be reproduced or transmitted, in any form or by any means, electronic, mechanical, photocopying, recording and otherwise, or stored in any retrieval system of any nature, without written permission."

Vested – Established by law as a permanent right. (What man can claim the rights to ownership of God's word?) The Bible called the King James "Authorized" Version was "Authorized" by the British Crown, not by God.